INTRODUCING
ISSUES WITH
OPPOSING
VIEWPOINTS®

Rap Music

Noah Berlatsky, *Book Editor*

GREENHAVEN PRESS
A part of Gale, Cengage Learning

GALE
CENGAGE Learning®

Detroit • New York • San Francisco • New Haven, Conn • Waterville, Maine • London

Elizabeth Des Chenes, *Director, Publishing Solutions*

For more information, contact:
Greenhaven Press
27500 Drake Rd.
Farmington Hills, MI 48331-3535
Or you can visit our Internet site at gale.cengage.com

For product information and technology assistance, contact us at

Gale Customer Support, 1-800-877-4253
For permission to use material from this text or product, submit all requests online at www.cengage.com/permissions

Further permissions questions can be e-mailed to permissionrequest@cengage.com

Articles in Greenhaven Press anthologies are often edited for length to meet page requirements. In addition, original titles of these works are changed to clearly present the main thesis and to explicitly indicate the author's opinion. Every effort is made to ensure that Greenhaven Press accurately reflects the original intent of the authors. Every effort has been made to trace the owners of copyrighted material.

Cover image © Kzenon/Shutterstock.com

LIBRARY OF CONGRESS CATALOGING-IN-PUBLICATION DATA

Rap music / Noah Berlatsky, book editor.
 p. cm. -- (Introducing issues with opposing viewpoints)
 Includes bibliographical references and index.
 ISBN 978-0-7377-6496-3 (hardcover)
 1. Rap (Music)--Social aspects. 2. Rap (Music)--Political aspects. I. Berlatsky, Noah.
 ML3918.R37R35 2012
 782.421649--dc23
                                                                    2012018753

Printed in the United States of America
1 2 3 4 5 6 7 16 15 14 13 12

Contents

Foreword   5

Introduction   7

Chapter 1: Does Rap Music Promote Violence?

1. Rap Music Glamorizes and Contributes to Gun Violence   11
   Warren Kinsella

2. Rap Music No Longer Glamorizes Prison as It Once Did   16
   David Dennis

3. Sharpton: Ban Artists Linked to Violence   21
   Nekesa Mumbi Moody

4. Rap Music Can Be Used to Promote Nonviolence   26
   Monse Sepulveda

5. Rap Music Reflects an African American Culture That
   Accepts Domestic Violence   32
   Brian Sims

6. The Rap Community Can Come Together to Reject
   Domestic Violence   41
   Bakari Kitwana

Chapter 2: Is Rap Music Harmful to Women?

1. Rap Music Contributes to Worldwide Harm to Women   47
   Liza Weisstuch

2. Rap Music Has a Long Tradition of Feminism   52
   Akoto Ofori-Atta

3. Men and Women Should Reject Misogynistic Rap   59
   Liz Funk

4. Hip-Hop Prison Culture Hurts Women   65
   Prison Culture

5. R&B Is More Harmful to Women than Rap   70
   Brandon Soderberg

6. R&B Can Teach Feminist Lessons   77
   Sarah Jaffe

Chapter 3: What Is the Political Effect of Rap Music?

1. Rap Music Is a Worldwide Form of Political Resistance   84
   Andalusia Knoll, with Scott Pinkelman

2. Rap Music Is Not Politically Thoughtful or Effective   91
   John H. McWhorter

3. Rap's Promotion of Capitalism and Success Is Dangerous   98
   Dreda Say Mitchell

4. Rap's Promotion of Capitalism and Success Is Healthy   103
   Steve Yates

Facts About Rap Music   109
Organizations to Contact   113
For Further Reading   117
Index   120
Picture Credits   126

Foreword

Indulging in a wide spectrum of ideas, beliefs, and perspectives is a critical cornerstone of democracy. After all, it is often debates over differences of opinion, such as whether to legalize abortion, how to treat prisoners, or when to enact the death penalty, that shape our society and drive it forward. Such diversity of thought is frequently regarded as the hallmark of a healthy and civilized culture. As the Reverend Clifford Schutjer of the First Congregational Church in Mansfield, Ohio, declared in a 2001 sermon, "Surrounding oneself with only like-minded people, restricting what we listen to or read only to what we find agreeable is irresponsible. Refusing to entertain doubts once we make up our minds is a subtle but deadly form of arrogance." With this advice in mind, Introducing Issues with Opposing Viewpoints books aim to open readers' minds to the critically divergent views that comprise our world's most important debates.

Introducing Issues with Opposing Viewpoints simplifies for students the enormous and often overwhelming mass of material now available via print and electronic media. Collected in every volume is an array of opinions that captures the essence of a particular controversy or topic. Introducing Issues with Opposing Viewpoints books embody the spirit of nineteenth-century journalist Charles A. Dana's axiom: "Fight for your opinions, but do not believe that they contain the whole truth, or the only truth." Absorbing such contrasting opinions teaches students to analyze the strength of an argument and compare it to its opposition. From this process readers can inform and strengthen their own opinions, or be exposed to new information that will change their minds. Introducing Issues with Opposing Viewpoints is a mosaic of different voices. The authors are statesmen, pundits, academics, journalists, corporations, and ordinary people who have felt compelled to share their experiences and ideas in a public forum. Their words have been collected from newspapers, journals, books, speeches, interviews, and the Internet, the fastest growing body of opinionated material in the world.

Introducing Issues with Opposing Viewpoints shares many of the well-known features of its critically acclaimed parent series, Opposing Viewpoints. The articles are presented in a pro/con format, allowing readers to absorb divergent perspectives side by side. Active reading questions preface each viewpoint, requiring the student to approach the material thoughtfully and carefully. Useful charts, graphs, and cartoons supplement each article. A thorough introduction provides readers with crucial background on an issue. An annotated bibliography points the reader toward articles, books, and websites that contain additional information on the topic. An appendix of organizations to contact contains a wide variety of charities, nonprofit organizations, political groups, and private enterprises that each hold a position on the issue at hand. Finally, a comprehensive index allows readers to locate content quickly and efficiently.

Introducing Issues with Opposing Viewpoints is also significantly different from Opposing Viewpoints. As the series title implies, its presentation will help introduce students to the concept of opposing viewpoints and learn to use this material to aid in critical writing and debate. The series' four-color, accessible format makes the books attractive and inviting to readers of all levels. In addition, each viewpoint has been carefully edited to maximize a reader's understanding of the content. Short but thorough viewpoints capture the essence of an argument. A substantial, thought-provoking essay question placed at the end of each viewpoint asks the student to further investigate the issues raised in the viewpoint, compare and contrast two authors' arguments, or consider how one might go about forming an opinion on the topic at hand. Each viewpoint contains sidebars that include at-a-glance information and handy statistics. A Facts About section located in the back of the book further supplies students with relevant facts and figures.

Following in the tradition of the Opposing Viewpoints series, Greenhaven Press continues to provide readers with invaluable exposure to the controversial issues that shape our world. As John Stuart Mill once wrote: "The only way in which a human being can make some approach to knowing the whole of a subject is by hearing what can be said about it by persons of every variety of opinion and studying all modes in which it can be looked at by every character of mind. No wise man ever acquired his wisdom in any mode but this." It is to this principle that Introducing Issues with Opposing Viewpoints books are dedicated.

Introduction

"Hip-hop has always been about speaking your mind and about breaking down barriers, but everyone in hip-hop discriminates against gay people. . . . I wanna just come on TV and just tell my rappers, tell my friends, 'Yo, stop it.'"

—Rapper Kanye West to MTV, August 2005

Rap music and hip-hop have often been accused of homophobia, or prejudice against gay people, particularly gay men. For example, Terrance Dean's book *Hiding in Hip Hop: On the Down Low in the Entertainment Industry—from Music to Hollywood* describes the author's experiences as a closeted gay man in hip-hop. In an April 6, 2011, article on the website Hello Beautiful, Dean summarized his assessment of rap music's attitude toward gay men:

> Hip Hop is a culture and environment which does not provide a safe place for an artist to come forward or to come out. If you listen to many rap lyrics they promote hate and gay-bashing. It is an environment where the thug and gangster mentality is prevalent. Artists boast of a hyper-masculine bravado, with their crotch-grabbing, degradation of women, and their braggadocios lyrical slaying [sic] about the number of women they've slept with and children they've produced. . . .
>
> There is a Don't Ask, Don't Tell policy, where the artists, executives, and fans do not want to know, or should I dare say, refuse to believe that a Hip Hop artist could be gay.

In April 2011 Mister Cee, a popular New York DJ at hip-hop radio station Hot 97, was arrested for public indecency when he was discovered having sex in a parked car with a young man. The incident sparked an extended public discussion in the hip-hop community about homosexuality and homophobia. Anyabwile Love, a PhD candidate at Temple University who teaches a class on the history of hip-hop, tried to talk about the incident with his students. Although students were willing to speculate about whether female rappers might be lesbians, they became silent when asked to talk about gay men in hip-hop. Love concluded that most of his students "seem to have been taught that to be a gay male means you're not a man," as quoted in an April 19, 2011, article on the website Colorlines. Love added that "homophobia is the last frontier [for discussion] in hip-hop."

Many rappers have recorded lyrics specifically targeting gay people. For example, Big Daddy Kane stated, "The Big Daddy law is anti-faggot," and Brand Nubian declared, "Don't understand their ways/ And I ain't down with gays." One artist who has frequently been accused of homophobia is the popular rapper Eminem. Eminem has often used the derogatory anti-gay term *faggot* in his lyrics and has also rapped about killing gay people. In his 2000 song "Criminal," Eminem stated:

Whether you're a fag or a lez
Or the homosex, hermaph or trans-a-vest
Pants or dress
Hate fags?
The answer's yes.

British gay rights activist Peter Tatchell was quoted in a February 5, 2001, BBC News article as saying that Eminem's "homophobic jibes help make bigotry cool and acceptable." Chris Clanks, in a December 4, 2009, post on the gay pop culture website AfterElton.com, noted that Eminem was still using anti-gay lyrics on his records. "Eminem's been around for ten years now," Clanks said. "Is this really the only way he can sell an album?"

Eminem responded to such accusations in an October 2011 interview with Anderson Cooper on the CBS News program *60 Minutes*. Eminem said that when he uses the word *faggot*, he is not specifically referring to gay people. He added, "I don't have any problem with nobody." He also argued that his popularity caused him to be singled out, though many other rappers use similar antigay language.

Some hip-hop artists have begun to speak out against homophobia. The female rapper Nicki Minaj, for example, recorded a 2010 video in which she spoke out against the bullying of gay youth. She urged gay teens not to commit suicide, telling her gay fans, "I love you very, very much," and stating, "For the people who don't love you, they need help."

Other rappers who have recently spoken out against homophobia include Fat Joe, who declared, "If you gay, you gay. That's your preference. F--- it if the people don't like it," and gangsta rapper Game, who said, "I don't have a problem with gay people." Lil B, who is heterosexual, called his 2011 album *I'm Gay (I'm Happy)*, sparking death threats. Lil B explained that he used that title because "I hope that I can turn some of my fans that might be homophobic or supporters that might be homophobic and say, 'You know what? We're all one people. This is love.'"

Writer Chris Lee, in a December 20, 2011, article on the Daily Beast website, speculated that rappers may be speaking out against homophobia in part for business reasons. Gay people are consumers just like heterosexual people, and hip-hop as a business wants to sell albums to them as well as to everyone else. In addition, some pop artists, like Lady Gaga, have had massive success through embracing a gay style and identity.

Lee also suggests that rappers may be more comfortable opposing homophobia now than in the past because of hip-hop's massive mainstream success. Rappers now have significant wealth and popular success, Lee says, and as a result, they "seem less compelled to define themselves against others as a means of self-validation than at any other point in hip-hop history."

Introducing Issues with Opposing Viewpoints: Rap Music looks at other connections between rap music and culture in chapters titled "Does Rap Music Promote Violence?," "Is Rap Music Harmful to Women?," and "What Is the Political Effect of Rap Music?" The authors in this volume express a variety of viewpoints about the positive and negative effects of rap music's effect on society's attitudes and prejudices.

Chapter 1

Does Rap Music Promote Violence?

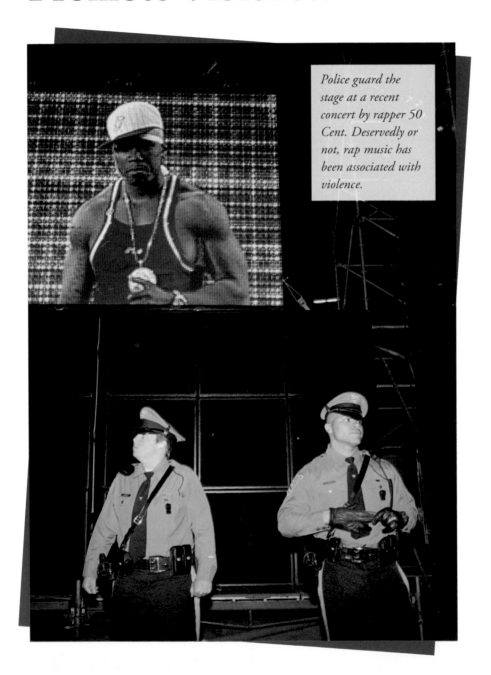

Police guard the stage at a recent concert by rapper 50 Cent. Deservedly or not, rap music has been associated with violence.

Viewpoint 1

Rap Music Glamorizes and Contributes to Gun Violence

Warren Kinsella

"After a while, the violence in such music almost denudes one of feeling."

Warren Kinsella is a blogger for the *National Post.* In the following viewpoint, he argues that rap music glamorizes gun culture. He says that studies show that the focus on guns in rap videos and lyrics can encourage violence among those who listen to the music. Kinsella does not advocate censorship but suggests that those involved in the rap music industry need to be more responsible. He also points out that the gun culture can hurt rap artists themselves, whose fascination with guns can get them in trouble with the law.

AS YOU READ, CONSIDER THE FOLLOWING QUESTIONS:
1. As reported in the viewpoint, how does the NWA video "Alwayz Into Somethin'" begin and end?
2. What excuses about gun violence did Rodrigo Bascunan hear from record executives and hip-hop artists?
3. Who is Alias Donmillion, according to Kinsella?

If you believe artists should strive to improve the human condition, don't go looking on the Internet for NWA's 1991 music video, "Alwayz Into Somethin." It is only likely to leave you feeling depressed.

Violence as Entertainment

NWA was short for Niggaz With Attitude, one of the pioneers of the now-crowded genre known as "gangsta rap." "Alwayz Into Somethin" has been described as one of the most violent music videos ever made.

A bloody store holdup kicks off the video, and a bloodier gang shoot-out ends it. In between, NWA's members point guns at the screen and fire at the viewer. "I got 44 ways of getting' paid," snarls Eazy E, holding up a .44 calibre handgun. "Sittin' in my lap as I roll off the Compton blocks? So I grab the nine and the clip, and go to murder motherfu--ers at night?" and so on. Such lyrics have become a cliché of the genre, but were then seen (and still should be seen) as shockingly violent.

After a while, the violence in such music almost denudes one of feeling. As with much of Hollywood, it serves up violence as entertainment, and glorifies gun culture. Does it have real-life implications?

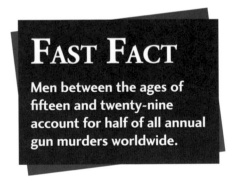

FAST FACT

Men between the ages of fifteen and twenty-nine account for half of all annual gun murders worldwide.

There are plenty of studies to suggest it does. One 1995 University of North Carolina research project, which examined "deleterious effects of rap music," exposed control groups of young men to violent and non-violent videos. Those shown the violent material "expressed greater acceptance of the use of violence [and] reported a higher probability that they would engage in violence." Many other studies have reached similar conclusions.

Rodrigo Bascunan—a co-owner of the foremost Canadian hip hop magazine, *Pound*—is not one to argue with the social scientists. While writing a fascinating new book with co-author Christian Pearce— *Enter the Babylon System: Unpacking Gun Culture from Samuel Colt to 50 Cent*—Bascunan heard the same excuses, repeatedly, from record company executives; and from hip hop artists themselves.

"When it served them, they would say that they were role models, and that they have positive influence," says Bascunan, who lives in Toronto, and resembles a rap artist himself. "And when it was going to be used in some negative manner, it became: 'Oh no, it's just entertainment. You need to raise your own kids.' But you can't have it both ways."

In the soon-to-be-released book, the authors avoid whitewashing the culture they write about in their popular magazine. "Few would deny that rap music plays a role in the problem with guns—especially not us," the pair writes. "[But] whatever blame is due some emcees for gun violence, at least as much is due outside of hip hop."

NWA's Easy E (pictured) has come under fire for promoting guns in his rap videos.

Seventeen Rap Songs with "Glock" in the Title

The Glock series of semiautomatic pistols was developed by Austrian gun designer Gaston Glock in the early 1980s. In addition to being conventional service weapons, a number of models are suitable for concealed carry.

Performer	Song
Three 6 Mafia	"Mask and da Glock" (1991)
Cypress Hill	"Hand on the Glock" (1993)
TRU	"Ain't No Glock" (1995)
Smoothe Da Hustler	"Glocks on Cock" (1996)
Mac Dre	"Maggots on My Glock" (1996)
Heather B.	"All Glocks Down" (1996)
Bone Thugs-N-Harmony	"Shots 2 da Double Glock" (1998)
Terror Squad	"Pass the Glock" (1999)
T.I.	"2 Glock 9s" (2000)
Wu-Tang Clan	"The Glock" (2001)
The RZA	"Glocko Pop" (2001)
2Pac	"2 Glocks" (2003)
Cee-lo	"Glockapella" (2004)
Los Tres Mosqueteros	"Con Mi Glock-Glock" (2004)
Juelz Santana	"Glock Pop!" (2005)
Papoose	"2 Glocks" (2005)
Lloyd Banks	"Without My Glock" (2006)

Taken from: Rodrigo Bascunan and Christian Pearce, *Enter the Babylon System: Unpacking Gun Culture from Samuel Colt to 50 Cent.* Toronto: Vintage Canada, 2007, p. 46.

Among those that bear blame, they write, are gun manufacturers, governments and media companies that "take financial advantage of a profound fascination with the image of guns."

The Babylon System
Enter the Babylon System—which takes its title from a 1979 Bob Marley lyric, decrying those who "suck the blood of the sufferers"—

is a gripping compendium of hip hop's "fascination with the image of guns." For example, a list is provided of nearly 60 rappers whose names refer to guns, like Three Glock, or AK-47. One chart details 17 rap songs with the word "Glock" [a kind of gun] in their title. Another one lists 13 songs titled, simply, "Bang Bang." It is simultaneously riveting and repulsive.

So, does hip hop deserve to be censored, as Tipper Gore [the wife of former vice president Al Gore] and others famously proposed in the mid-1980s, when the gangsta rap genre was scandalizing middle America? Bascunan opposes that, pointing out that censorship will simply make violent hip hop seem more like an outlaw culture and therefore more attractive to the white suburban males who listen to it the most.

The issue became somewhat more than hypothetical in Toronto this week [in December 2006], when local rapper Alias Donmillion pleaded guilty to three firearms charges and was sentenced to more than two years' imprisonment. Alias—with a new album, a new single and a new video in rotation on Much Music—pleaded guilty to firing a .380 calibre semi-automatic handgun on a downtown street. When caught by police, he had the gun, spent shell casings and almost 11 grams of crack. It was, he told a reporter over a phone line at the Don Jail [in Toronto], a "dumb" thing to do.

Of that there is no doubt. But when Donmillion gets out of jail and heads to the studio to record his next album, will he confess his dumbness and decry drug-and-gun gangsta culture? Or will he bask in his real-life criminal bona fides and turn his incarceration into a NWA style gangland epic? I think we all know the answer.

EVALUATING THE AUTHOR'S ARGUMENTS:

Author Warren Kinsella reports that Rodrigo Bascunan thinks that rap music should not be censored. What is Bascunan's argument? Do you agree with him? Do you think that the argument also applies to adult content warnings on rap albums? Why or why not?

Rap Music No Longer Glamorizes Prison as It Once Did

"Now, getting arrested for a rapper is the same as getting arrested for a teacher, janitor or politician. It's a bad move."

David Dennis

David Dennis is a writer whose work has appeared in the *Smoking Section*, the *Source*, and numerous other publications. In the following viewpoint, he argues that being arrested and going to jail used to be a boost for a rap artist's career. He says that now, however, rap music has become a mainstream industry and going to jail means a loss of career opportunities. Dennis says that this may be a positive development, because it will show fans that criminal activities are self-destructive rather than glamorous.

AS YOU READ, CONSIDER THE FOLLOWING QUESTIONS:
1. What happened to the protagonist in *Hustle and Flow*, and why does Dennis say this is unrealistic in 2010?
2. Why does the author say that nobody cared when the news broke that Ja Rule was going to jail?
3. What is the bright side to the fact that jail is no longer a career boost for rappers, according to Dennis?

*H*ustle and Flow [a 2005 film focusing on the rap industry] had a decidedly Hollywood ending. Instead of the more realistic conclusion of having the protagonist's Hip-Hop dreams end in a cloud of dust like most other wannabe lyricists, [the film's main character] Djay . . . saw his fame rise to superstar levels almost solely because he beat up a rapper and ended up in jail. In 2005

Now that rap has gone mainstream, controversial rappers have more to lose. Rapper T.I. (pictured) suffered the loss of endorsements, movie roles, and income after his arrest for probation violation in 2010.

this was relatively realistic; after all 50 Cent had just broken records for his debut album hot off the heels of getting shot nine times. Ever since 2Pac [Tupac Shakur, an important rap artist who was shot and killed in 1996] wrote the blueprint for "street cred," run-ins with the law, shootouts and jail time were precursors to stardom. At some point, that *Hustle and Flow* logic became obsolete. Now, getting arrested for a rapper is the same as getting arrested for a teacher, janitor or politician. It's a bad move.

Hip-Hop Is Mainstream

[American rap artist] T.I.'s legal troubles through the years illuminate this change. Right after Tip's [T.I.'s] first commercially successful album *Trap Muzik* dropped, he was arrested for violating his probation stemming from a 1997 arrest. Suddenly, T.I.'s street tales were substantiated, adding to his urban legend. Fast forward to 2010 and T.I.'s current incarceration has turned the court of public opinion against him. This court includes faithful T.I. fans that can recite every one of his trap tales and "f**k the police" bars. The fact is, and please don't be disappointed by this spoiler alert, Hip-Hop is mainstream. The genre is a multi-billion dollar industry that's much more integrated into the American lore than it was 15 years ago. When 2Pac went to jail, he faced album pushbacks and a couple of lost movie roles.

> **FAST FACT**
>
> Tupac Shakur, an influential gangsta rapper who was shot and killed in 1996, is one of the best-selling rappers in history, with more than 75 million albums sold.

T.I. went to jail and he lost endorsements, movie roles and likely millions of dollars in other opportunities. When T.I. went to jail for smoking weed in his car, he was seen as an idiot.

Which brings us to Hip-Hop's most recent inmate-to-be, Ja Rule. When the news broke that Ja was sentenced to two years in jail, nobody really cared. It was just another sign that Ja's career was over. The former star had it all at one point: starring in movies multiplatinum albums and writing melodies for J. Lo. A poorly-executed

Cartoon copyright © by Eason Gallery Studios. Reproduced by permission.

beef with 50 Cent and a drastic decline in music quality resulted in an epic career homicide. There was a time when a rapper's arrest could have provided a shot in the arm for a career. While it's clear that there isn't much that will give Ja any level of relevance, jail definitely won't do the trick. Instead, it's just the final casket close to a career that ended years ago.

Unfortunately, Ja Rule seemed to not relish the fact that he was in the public spotlight for a few minutes.

"Jail Means It's Over"

He took to his Twitter: "minor setback for a major comeback." If only it were that easy. Jail means it's over for Ja.

It's a shame that the clink isn't the career boost it used to be. But there is a bright side: we're all worried about the influence Hip-Hop has on our kids. Granted, our children's idols going to jail as often as they go to the club isn't the best-case scenario, but having these stars come out of it sans [without] millions and testifying to the fact that the experience was horrible, will act as much more of a deterrent than the "yeah, I served that time without a problem" attitude of the Hip-Hop Medieval Times. Maybe Ja Rule can find solace in his ability to act as an example for the youth. Especially once he realizes he's unlikely to find it in hopes of a reborn music career.

> ### EVALUATING THE AUTHOR'S ARGUMENTS:
>
> Tupac Shakur, a famous and influential rapper who many said glorified violence and the gangster lifestyle, was shot and killed in 1996. Yet after the shooting, rappers and fans continued to glamorize violence in rap. Do you think that arrests and career troubles will have a stronger effect on deglamorizing violence, as David Dennis suggests? Why or why not?

Sharpton: Ban Artists Linked to Violence

"But he [Reverend Al Sharpton] did say there should be a process in which violent acts involving rap acts are punished by denying them publicity on the airwaves."

Nekesa Mumbi Moody

Nekesa Mumbi Moody is a writer for AP Online. In the following viewpoint, Moody discusses Al Sharpton's argument that hip hop is embedded in a culture of violence. Sharpton contends that rappers, like 50 Cent and The Game, encourage and perpetuate violence and should receive a punishment for doing so. He claims that there should be a process in which violent rap acts, such as the shooting between 50 Cent and The Game, are punished by denying them publicity.

AS YOU READ, CONSIDER THE FOLLOWING QUESTIONS:
1. According to Sharpton, what incident demonstrated the need for a policy to ban rappers who engage in violence?
2. Who was 50 Cent's former protégé, according to Moody?
3. What was rapper Lil' Kim on trial for, as reported by the author?

The Rev. Al Sharpton is putting in his two cents about the latest drama involving 50 Cent. The civil rights leader on Tuesday proposed a ban that would muzzle artists who are connected to any violent acts, denying them airplay on radio and television for 90 days.

Though Sharpton did not single out 50 Cent by name, he told The Associated Press that a recent shooting linked to a feud involving 50 demonstrated the need for such a policy.

"There's a difference in the having the right to express yourself and in engaging in violence and using the violence to hype record sales, and then polluting young Americans that this is the key to success, by gunslinging and shooting," he said.

Whether or not that's been the key to 50's success, he's certainly having a lot of it these days.

50 Cent is poised to debut at No. 1 on next week's album charts with his new album, "The Massacre." The follow-up to his 2003 debut, "Get Rich or Die Tryin'"—which sold 8 million copies—"The Massacre" is on track to sell about 1 million copies in just four days. In addition, he's got the nation's No. 1 single with "Candy Shop."

It comes a week after a bitter feud broke out involving the rapper and his former protégé, The Game. A member of The Game's crew was wounded during a shooting outside a New York hip-hop radio station, where 50 Cent—who produced part of The Game's platinum-selling debut album—was on the air, announcing that he was kicking him out of his G-Unit clique.

No one has been arrested for the shooting, and police are still investigating the incident, but some in the media have suggested it may have been the beginning of violent dispute between the two rappers, who flaunt a gangsta image: Both are former drug dealers and both have been shot multiple times. There have been comparisons to the feud between Tupac Shakur and the Notorious B.I.G. nearly a decade ago; both rappers were shot to death in separate slayings that have not been solved.

Perhaps coincidentally, rapper Lil' Kim is on trial for perjury and conspiracy in connection with another shooting that occurred outside the same hip-hop station in 2001. Lil' Kim is accused of lying about the incident to protect the alleged shooters.

Meanwhile, *Newsweek* reported this week that the federal government is investigating the entire rap industry for alleged crimes;

Violence is common in the rap community. A sympathy card forms part of an on-site memorial in Inglewood, California, where rapper M-Bone was killed in a drive-by shooting in 2011.

Percentage Change in Murder Rate by Race, 2001–2007

This graph comes from a Northeastern University report released in December 2008, which, as the *Wall Street Journal* explains, shows a significant increase in the number of African American teens who were the victims of violent crime.

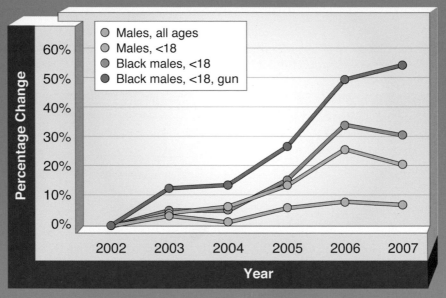

Legend:
- Males, all ages
- Males, <18
- Black males, <18
- Black males, <18, gun

Taken from: Postbourgie, "We Gotta Put Our Heads Together and Stop the Violence," www.posbourgie.com. Based on data from James Alan Fox and Marc L. Swatt, "The Recent Surge in Homicides Involving Young Black Males and Guns: Time to Reinvest in Prevention and Crime Control," Northeastern University Press, December 2008.

already, Irv Gotti, head of The Inc. label, was arrested earlier this year on money laundering charges. A federal indictment alleges the label, home to Ja Rule and Ashanti, was part of a murderous criminal enterprise that protected its interstate crack and heroin operation with calculated street assassinations.

Sharpton stressed that he was not targeting 50 Cent or The Game in his new crusade, and noted he did not know what role, if any, the two had in the shooting. But he did say there should be a process in which violent acts involving rap acts are punished by denying them publicity on the airwaves.

"The whole body politic of America addressed Janet Jackson's breast, and it didn't hurt anybody," he said of the infamous Super

Bowl flashing. "Here you have actual bloodshed, and people are not even responding at federally regulated radio stations. . . . black kids are expected to shoot each other, and nobody cares? Well I care, and I think somebody should do something about it."

A request for comment to Universal Music Group—the parent company of 50 Cent's label Interscope—was not immediately returned, nor was a request put into MTV or Sony BMG.

A representative for Hot 97 (WQHT-FM in New York) said the radio station meets Federal Communications Commission standards.

"We in no way condone acts of violence," station spokesman Alex Dudley said. "We hope that the perpetrators of these violent acts are prosecuted to the fullest extent of the law by the proper authorities."

Bryan Leach, a vice president at TVT Records (home to platinum-selling rappers such as Lil Jon and the East Side Boyz and the Ying Yang Twins), said he wasn't sure Sharpton's proposal was the right way to resolve rap-related violence. But he conceded the issue needed to be addressed.

"I think we can be vocal and I think we can show people that it's something that concerns us just like piracy concerns us," he said. "Violence in songs and violence in terms of how it translates in society, in particular the black community, is something that concerns a large part of the record industry."

Leach said he was also concerned that the media was sensationalizing the events of the past week and potentially inflaming the situation.

"A lot of it doesn't seem to be coming from people who really understand the history, really understand the parties involved, really understand a lot of the facts," he said.

EVALUATING THE AUTHOR'S ARGUMENTS:

Do you agree with Al Sharpton's belief, as reported by Mekesa Mumbi Moody, that denying violent rappers publicity would help reduce the violence? Explain your answer.

Rap Music Can Be Used to Promote Nonviolence

"Trasciende has taken hip-hop, an art form associated [with] masculinity, and uses it to fervently argue that there are men . . . who strive to live a life of nonviolence."

Monse Sepulveda

Monse Sepulveda is a Chilean student at Soka University of America in Aliso Viejo, California. She is researching Guatemalan youth and violence. In the following viewpoint, she says that Guatemala is suffering from an epidemic of violence, especially among youth. She says a government crackdown on violence may simply result in more violence and death. Sepulveda reports on an organization called Trasciende, which uses hip-hop and rap to promote nonviolence among youth.

AS YOU READ, CONSIDER THE FOLLOWING QUESTIONS:
  1. According to Sepulveda, what is the murder rate in Guatemala, and how does that compare with rates in the United States and Mexico?
  2. As reported in the viewpoint, who is Otto Perez Molin and what does he suggest doing to address violence in Guatemala?
  3. What four values does Mr. Fer say that Trasciende promotes?

This summer [2011], as I was sipping coffee with a friend in downtown Guatemala City, I was introduced to a news reporter who agreed to take me with him as he visited murder sites. The next day I arrived at his office at 6 A.M. and immediately we received our first call: a young man with signs of torture had been shot and thrown down a ravine, his hands and feet tied. In the next thirteen hours, we received twelve such calls.

Guatemala and Violence

Guatemala is nowadays one of the most violent countries in Latin America, with an average of 45 murders per 100,000 people each year. (By comparison, the homicide rate in the US stands at about 5 per 100,000 and in Mexico it was 22 per 100,000 last year). Most of these murders are attributed to gang violence, especially males. This notion is supported by continuous reports of the brutality of gang violence and by the fact that 90% of the people murdered were males under the age of 29. Indeed, male youth in Guatemala are committing atrocious acts of violence, but blame now falls indiscriminately upon all youth. Tattoos, piercings and a fashion style that looks very much like US rap artists, are now considered the "markers" of violence. As a result, the youth in Guatemala suffer from a dangerous stigmatization that places them in a vulnerable position when confronted by the police and angry mobs. This prevents many of them from making their way into society and fails to acknowledge that these youth are victims to violence themselves. Moreover, it encourages police to use brutality with impunity and promotes a disregard for the legal process.

Guatemala is about to elect a new president this coming November [2011], and the two people now contesting are Otto Perez Molina and Manuel Baldizon. Both candidates have centered their campaigns on the concern for public security and advocate a stronger government stance against crime. More specifically, Perez Molina proposes a program known as "Iron Fist," which has already been implemented in El Salvador (where it's known as "Super Iron Fist") and in Mexico. The core of this program is to increase police and military involvement in the persecution of drug traffickers and gang members or people suspected to be involved. However, both in Mexico and El Salvador this caused an explosion of violence and murders, which Mexicans will often refer to as a "war." Accordingly, indiscriminate violence amongst the youth as well as against them has increased. The programs put

During Guatemala's presidential race, Otto Perez Molina—pictured here on November 6, 2011, after winning the election—had made a campaign promise to take an "iron fist" approach to prosecuting drug traffickers and street gangs.

forward by both candidates can only have the same negative impact, because violence foments more violence. I am afraid that no matter what the outcome of the election is, the youth of Guatemala will suffer even more in the coming years.

Promoting Nonviolence

In the context of this reality one would not expect the youth to organize nonviolent actions, workshops or, as we shall see, an academy that teaches the principles of nonviolence. Yet, if we were to take a stroll down Calle 12 and 6ta Avenida, of Zone 1 in Guatemala City, we would find a group of mostly young men who celebrate the spirit of nonviolence every day.

Trasciende, an organization founded in 2009 by a group of five B-boys (break dancers), is a hip-hop academy that offers art workshops as a means to draw the youth away from violence and into a peaceful environment. Mr. Fer, the head of the academy, meets regularly with those who attend the workshops to discuss the four values Trasciende promotes—Peace, Love, Unity and Enjoyment—and how these can bring about real social and political change if only we commit to them fully. Mr. Fer told me he thinks Trasciende is now transforming into a bridge for the youth, especially men, who live in "territories owned by enemy gangs. They are starting to understand the core of the problem: that they have been driven to believe in false differences between them." When asked what he believes is the solution to the violence in Guatemala he responded, "I can help by not helping violence. I will refrain from feeding my own humanity to the pool of blood already existing. And I hope I can inspire more youth to do the same."

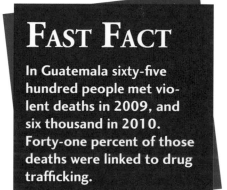

FAST FACT

In Guatemala sixty-five hundred people met violent deaths in 2009, and six thousand in 2010. Forty-one percent of those deaths were linked to drug trafficking.

Aware of the escalating demand for military interventionism in the problem of gang violence and the potential threat to the youth, Trasciende has started to organize more venues to encourage the youth to join this hip-hop movement: national dancing competitions,

Homicides in Latin America, 2000–2008

Number of Homicides per 100,000 Inhabitants			
Country	2000	2008	% Change 2000–2008
Argentina	7.0	5.3	-24.7
Bolivia	3.7	10.6	183.4
Brazil	26.7	25.2	-5.6
Chile	1.9	1.7	-10.5
Colombia	63.3	39.0	-38.4
Costa Rica	6.3	11.0	74.6
Ecuador	15.3	18.0	17.6
El Salvador	37.3	52.0	39.4
Guatemala	25.8	48.0	86.0
Honduras	49.9	57.9	16.0
Mexico	14.0	12.0	-14.3
Nicaragua	9.0	13.0	44.4
Panama	10.1	19.0	89.6
Paraguay	12.6	12.2	-3.2
Peru	4.9	11.2	128.6
Dominican Republic	13.1	21.5	64.2
Uruguay	4.6	5.8	26.1
Venezuela	33.0	47.2	43
Latin America	18.8	22.8	21.3

Taken from: Inter-American Institute of Human Rights, 2010. www.iidh.ed.cr/multic/defaultIIDHEn.aspx?Portal=IIDHen.

graffiti and emceeing workshops and scholarships to compete overseas. Trasciende has taken hip-hop, an art form associated [with] masculinity, and uses it to fervently argue that there are men, thousands of them, who strive to live a life of nonviolence, challenging the notion of masculinity as intrinsically violent. "It is not ironic," Mr. Fer said, "that those who are most heavily stigmatized are the ones refusing to be violent. It is simply perceived as an irony by those who perpetuate it. . . . But we will not buy into that irony; we will make sure everybody understands this." In spite of the threat of increasing persecution of the youth and the number of advocates of this movement that have already been killed, Mr. Fer, Trasciende and the youth continue to insist that the best way to start solving the problems of Guatemala is to make the decision to abstain from being a part of the perpetual cycle of violence.

EVALUATING THE AUTHOR'S ARGUMENTS:

Monse Sepulveda argues that violence leads to more violence. Do you agree or disagree that increased policing and a crackdown on drug trafficking and gangs will result in more violence? Explain your reasoning.

Rap Music Reflects an African American Culture That Accepts Domestic Violence

"Black men have essentially been forced to hate the women they love and love the women they hate."

Brian Sims

Brian Sims is a professor of psychology at North Carolina Agricultural and Technical State University. In the following viewpoint, he argues that black men have a profound mistrust of black women that is used as a cultural justification for domestic violence. This mistrust is based on the ways black men and women were forced to view and interact with one another during slavery, he contends. Contemporary hip-hop reflects this deeply fractured relationship, according to Sims.

Brian Sims, "Get Your Mind Right: Domestic Violence," *HipHopDX,* March 3, 2009. www.hiphopdx.com. Reproduced by permission.

AS YOU READ, CONSIDER THE FOLLOWING QUESTIONS:
1. According to the author, what is social learning theory?
2. What criteria does Sims say a woman needs to meet in contemporary hip-hop if she is to be accepted by black men?
3. What percentage of Americans personally know someone who is or has been a victim of domestic violence, according to Sims?

In college I used to joke around with one of my teammates about how he was going to end up beating the shit out of his future wife one day. He was suave; ladies loved him. Still do. But his womanizing ways made all of us wonder how long it would be until some woman did something bad enough for him to choke her or slap her or whatever.

The Most Violent Society

We live in arguably the most violent society in the history of the world. Sure, the Romans had The Coliseum; but Americans have turned violence into a science. Literally. Americans are soaked with literal violence every day. Cartoons are violent. Video games are violent. There is violence on television, violence at the movie theater, violence on the radio and violence in the newspaper. So, although we love to ask questions about why there is violence in the home, the better question (to me) is how could there not be violence in the home?

From a psychological perspective, domestic violence is complex. Definitions vary, but most folks agree that when violence manifests itself in family or friendship circles, the term domestic violence applies.

One of the interesting things about rap music is its tendency to bring out the critic in people. Carl Jung, the famous Swiss psychiatrist once said "Everything that irritates us about others can lead us to an understanding of ourselves." I believe that he was on to something, mainly because as individuals we are all influenced by one another. No one lives in a vacuum. On a philosophical level, one's actions are not really one's own actions—they are really just reactions to an earlier action provided by someone else.

This immediately brings Hip Hop music and culture into the discussion, because Hip Hop is nothing more than one particular reaction to oppression and marginalization. At its core, Hip Hop was founded on the rejection of mainstream modes of thought, dress, dance and art. Without the ghetto, Hip Hop never would have existed.

"*But wait*," you say, "how is it that the rejection looks so much like the original?" A close look at early Hip Hop may provide some answers.

"Don't Push Me"

"You'll grow in the ghetto, living second rate
And your eyes will sing a song of deep hate"

The Furious Five's words from "The Message" capture the essence of life lived in the atrocity of sheer poverty. The verses illustrate the weird realities of hood life—events and scenes that simply don't make sense until you live them. But the song's true brilliance lives in the hook, which reveals the real issue.

"Don't push me, 'cause I'm close to the edge"
("You don't have to do anything to mess me up; I'm already on the verge of destruction.")

I'm trying not to lose my head
("Simply trying to live is killing me.")

"It's like a jungle sometimes it makes me wonder how I keep from going under"
("It's a miracle that I have not been consumed by the craziness already.")

"The Message" (and countless other early Hip Hop narratives) acknowledges the fact that even though individuals may perpetuate madness, violence, hate, etc; the real issue is the societal circumstances that produce such problematic behavior. Which is all the more startling once you consider how things got to be the way they are. To quote [from a song by American rapper] Nas: "*It's elementary; they want us all gone eventually.*"

Social learning theory describes how individuals learn how they should behave by observing other people's behaviors and the consequences of their behaviors. In a nutshell, the individual is influenced by personal factors (e.g. emotion), environmental factors, and behavioral factors (e.g. smoking) that all interact to determine learning. A key construct in social learning theory is modeling. Modeling refers to the process of learning by observation, in a monkey-see, monkey-do sort of paradigm. So then, if, as a society, we've collectively learned to be violent, who have we learned such behavior from?

The easy answer is of course: "the media." As pointed out earlier, there is violence all over the airwaves. But perhaps this is a lazy answer as well. Maybe, if we were to examine ourselves, we would see that violence isn't just preached to us from a media minister behind a propaganda pulpit; it lives inside of us, calling out for redemption.

FAST FACT

According to the American Bar Association, the leading cause of death for black women between the ages of fifteen and thirty-four is homicide committed by a former or current intimate partner.

But domestic violence is even more complicated than that. It is easy enough to see how one might resort to violence against a known, clear adversary. It is another thing altogether to explain the mentality of someone who lashes out against his own loved ones. Perhaps the answer lies in perception. What if the aggressor actually perceives the loved one to be an enemy?

Love and Pride

Much of what really happened during America's period of chattel slavery has been lost, perhaps never to be found or brought to light again. But what we do know tells us that in many ways, black men were taught (in fact, in most cases forced) to view and treat his black feminine counterpart with distrust, aggression, hostility, and violence. Life on the plantation for women ranged from hell to hell, with hell in between. They were pressured to live the life of the exposed double-agent: constantly pandering to her white masters for mere survival while simultaneously clinging to her black male counterparts for humanity and sanity.

One result of this fractured version of community and all of the roles that came along with it was that the black woman was forced to do things that her black man hated. Like f--- the master and bear his children. Like feed the master and nurse his babies. Like worship the master and value his property.

It is not difficult for me to see how generations of black men forced to endure such reality might come to mistake their sisters for their enemies. The assault on black masculinity was (is) so pervasive that it warped men's minds enough to turn them against their one shot at freedom: Love.

Thus, a little over 100 years post-emancipation we are still witnessing the effects of black love on life support. In his reaction to white supremacy the black man has done exactly what the black woman has done: the only thing he could. When faced with a reality of having to deal with used up, f---ked up, sneaky, plotting, selfish women he began to acknowledge those aspects of her persona and accept her, albeit on a conditional basis. This explains beautifully why, in much of contemporary Hip Hop, the woman is only appropriated if she meets certain criteria—the most important of these being loyalty.

Rap music is filled with the construct of female loyalty. Rappers love glorifying women who are loyal or "ride or die" and castigating women who can't be trusted to stick around, despite any and all circumstances. We see it on The Notorious B.I.G.'s "Me and My Bitch":

"*But you was my bitch, the one who'd never snitch*
Love me when I'm broke or when I'm filthy f---in' rich."

And on 2Pac's "I Ain't Mad Atcha":

"*Rewind us back, to a time was much too young to know*
I caught a felony lovin' the way the guns blow
And even though we separated, you said that you'd wait
Don't give nobody no coochie while I be locked up state. . . .
You's a damned-ass bitch, but I aint mad atcha."

And on Jay-Z's "Song Cry":

"Shit I'm a man with pride, you don't do shit like that
You don't just pick up and leave and leave me sick like that
You don't throw away what we had, just like that
I was just f---in' them girls, I was gon' get right back."

These and thousands of verses like them are profound considering the affectionate use of the term "bitch" and the attribution of value to the woman based almost exclusively on her allegiance to an often undeserving man. Busta Rhymes, Snoop Dogg, 50 Cent, Big Pun, Ludacris, and countless other artists have songs about loving "bitches." I would argue that the term "bitch" itself represents the paradoxical duality inherent in loving someone that you are forced to hate. Black men have essentially been forced to hate the women they love and love the women they hate.

Many female rappers, such as Missy Elliot (pictured), refer to themselves as "bitches."
Such references, many believe, help to perpetuate domestic violence against women in the
African American community.

Women on some levels embrace it as well. Lil' Kim's moniker of "Queen B" actually refers to her posture as the "Queen Bitch." Missy Elliot has referred to herself as a bitch, as have Trina, Foxy Brown, Eve, and a long list of female emcees. Consider the psychological trauma that one must go through in order to use a verbal weapon like "bitch" as a term of endearment. And "bitch" is just the beginning! Our Hip Hop lexicon assaults women on a constant basis. Look at all of the sexual lingo that connotes violent imagery. "Beat," "cut," "stab," "smash," and "hit" are all colloquial euphemisms for sex. I still don't know what the proper name for "wife beater" is.

Unfortunately, as we shall see, it is not a large leap to go from verbal assault to physical assault.

Emotional and Physical Abuse

According to 2006 statistics, nearly three out of four (74%) Americans personally know someone who is or has been a victim of domestic violence, and approximately 30% of Americans say they know a woman who has been physically abused by her husband or boyfriend in the past year. These statistics are higher in the black community. The *Journal of Family Violence* reported in 1990 that 72% of abuse victims felt that emotional abuse was harder to endure than physical abuse, and research suggests a direct link between verbal abuse and later physical abuse in relationships.

If we return to B.I.G.'s "Me and My Bitch," we get a clear admission of just how direct the link can be.

> *"And I admit, when the time is right, the wine is right*
> *I treat you right, you talk slick, I beat you right."*

I have heard theories of domestic violence that say that because Black men have been marginalized by society and denied personal autonomy, they may be prone to essentially "taking it out" on their women. Author Kevin Powell for instance, calls this phenomenon "bootleg masculinity." I'm not convinced that this explanation holds. Look at what Biggie is saying. "*Everything could be fine; but guess what: as soon as you mess up, that's your ass.*"

I have not heard anyone ever criticize the late great Christopher Wallace [Notorious B.I.G.'s birth name] for this sentiment. Nor am I out to do so here. My point is that maybe the reason why a 300 pound black man gets a pass for rapping about beating his woman "right" is because we silently acknowledge that he is touching on a deep, sore wound inflicted on us all during slavery.

I do not advocate silently dealing with this issue. We ought to talk about it in the open. Sure, I regret joking about domestic violence with my old teammate, but I do think that our open and honest discussions about how women can make us want to explode were healthy and proactive. And for what it is worth, we were wrong about him (as far as I know). But talking about domestic violence is difficult as long as we continue to blame the victim.

Mark Anthony Neal, associate professor in the Black Popular Culture Program in African and African American Studies at Duke has pointed out how Hip Hop is not the first black art form to contain violence towards women. According to Neal, the black legacy of violence includes notable figures like James Brown, Jackie Wilson, Patti LaBelle, Ike and Tina Turner and others. Hip Hop is not causing anything. It is reflecting.

Cartoon by Kevin Moore. www.Mooretoons.com. Reproduced by permission.

Which is why I was not surprised to read that Rihanna is going back to Chris Brown.[1] There are probably multiple reasons why battered women go back to the men who abuse them. Rihanna's example says that money, fame and celebrity have nothing to do with the psychology of abuse. Perhaps she went back because she felt the same pressure that untold millions of black women felt before her; to love her man in spite of himself.

> ## EVALUATING THE AUTHOR'S ARGUMENTS:
>
> Brian Sims argues that black male antagonism toward black women extends back to relationships during slavery. What evidence does he provide for this view, if any? What other kinds of evidence might he have used to make his argument more convincing?

---

1. In 2009 hip-hop and R&B star Brown assaulted his girlfriend, Rihanna, a singer in the same genres.

The Rap Community Can Come Together to Reject Domestic Violence

"This energy should be channeled into the creation of a concrete national agenda committed to ending domestic violence."

Bakari Kitwana

Bakari Kitwana is the coauthor of *Hip-Hop Activism in the Obama Era* and is a visiting scholar at Columbia College's Institute for the Study of Women and Gender in the Arts and Media. In the following viewpoint, he says that activism around hip-hop and rap music was important in organizing young people to vote for Barack Obama in the 2008 presidential election. Kitwana now believes that this energy should be channeled into organizing youth against domestic violence and abuse. He argues that this would reduce violence against women and also show the moral and political potential of hip-hop.

For nearly an entire week [in March 2009], the Chris Brown/ Rihanna alleged abuse incident[1] has dominated major news media headlines. Unfortunately, these sensationalized reports did less to elucidate the national epidemic of violence against women and more to cement into our national psyche the idea that the new face of domestic abuse is young, Black and hip-hop. Instead of accepting sole responsibility for one of America's most neglected pathologies, young Americans should turn this tragedy into an opportunity.

The Potential of Hip-Hop Activism

In the last two election cycles, hip-hop led the way in making involvement in national elections fashionable among youth. Hip-hop political organizers could do the same in extending that influence into the arena of public policy with the goal of establishing an innovative solution to abuse that shifts the way the nation thinks about its treatment of women.

The election of President Barack Obama, with young people across race supporting him long before even the African American community's vote was solidified, marked the first political victory for this generation. Two-thirds of the 23 million young Americans 18–29 who voted in the 2008 presidential election voted for Barack Obama. These same young people taking the lead on a public policy solution to end dating violence would be an important second act.

Contrary to public opinion the hip-hop community has a long history of resisting the status quo of domestic abuse, misogyny and gen-

1. Hip-hop and R&B star Brown assaulted his girlfriend, Rihanna, a singer in the same genres.

der inequity. From books like Tracy Sharpley-Whiting's *Pimps Up, Hos Down* and films like Aishah Simmons' *No! The Rape Documentary* to organizations like the Center for Young Women's Development and Industry Ears, Inc., there is an emerging hip-hop generation leadership that has its finger on the pulse of a change agenda for women.

Such an agenda is reflected in the nearly 5000 comments posted on Blackplanet.com responding to Chris Brown and Rihanna news one.com updates. The overwhelming mood of these comments was that the Black community needed to separate itself from stereotypes of domestic violence. Blackplanet.com members even spontaneously created online discussion groups to address the issue.

The media's obsession with the Chris Brown/Rihanna incident, alongside a new administration that seems to take the debt it owes young voters seriously, offers young political organizers a rare opportunity for this generation to take the lead on dating and domestic abuse.

Convicted of assaulting his girlfriend, singer Rihanna, Chris Brown (center) arrives at court to be sentenced. Sensationalized media reports helped fuel the belief that the new face of domestic violence is black and hip-hop.

Ending Domestic Violence

Although hip-hop didn't create America's gender problem, its mainstream dominant representations certainly helped reinforce it. Today's young Americans—especially those in the Chris Brown and Rihanna age group and the legions of even younger fans who idolize them—have come of age consuming a steady diet of these images. Few would argue that they are healthier or wiser as a result.

At the same time, there are very few places in our culture where we require young men to learn appropriate behavior for engaging their female counterparts, especially when relationships turn sour. (Rhode Island and Virginia law for high school instruction on dating are rare exceptions.) This advancing the status quo, alongside our failure as a society to entrench a workable solution into the fabric of our culture, is a deadly combination.

A recent report from the Bureau of Justice found that 1 in 3 girls in the US is a victim of physical, emotional or verbal abuse from a dating partner. 13 percent of teen girls say they were physically hurt or hit and 40 percent of teenage girls 14–17 years old say they know someone their age that has been hit by a boyfriend. And a 2003 nationwide survey from the Center for Disease Control of 15,000 9–12 grade high school students found that nearly 9 percent experienced physical dating violence, with rates among Black females (14 percent) nearly twice their white counterparts (7 percent). The rate for Latino females was 9.3 percent.

Now is not the time for young people inspired during the last election cycle to fall back into complacency. Instead this energy should be channeled into the creation of a concrete national agenda committed to ending domestic violence.

This certainly will require an institutional approach. In the same way that sex education worked its way into our schools, we need a similar curriculum from the earliest grades upward to change the ways Americans think about dating violence, domestic abuse and gender equity. At a bare minimum, this curriculum must teach boys that physical and emotional violence toward their girlfriends or any boys or men toward women is never an option.

Such a move would have several benefits: it would help create the major societal shift needed to curtail violence against women; it would allow hip-hop to reveal to the world that it has a moral center; and it would solidify a new movement for a new generation. All are important steps on the road to transforming America into a country that reflects, more accurately than our media representations, the generation currently preparing to inherit it.

EVALUATING THE AUTHOR'S ARGUMENTS:

Bakari Kitwana argues that hip-hop has a history of opposing domestic abuse, misogyny, and gender inequality. Would Brian Sims, the author of the previous viewpoint, agree with this view? How do songs such as Notorious B.I.G.'s "Me and My Bitch," which Sims discusses in the previous viewpoint, affect Kitwana's argument? Which do you think would be more important in shaping young people's attitudes, rap lyrics or the new school classes on dating that Kitwana recommends? Explain your answers.

Chapter 2

Is Rap Music Harmful to Women?

Hip-hop mogul Russell Simmons has called on the recording and broadcast industries to ban racial and sexual epithets from rap songs.

Viewpoint

1

Rap Music Contributes to Worldwide Harm to Women

Liza Weisstuch

"Hip-hop culture hasn't always been as sexist as it is now."

Liza Weisstuch is a contributor to the *Christian Science Monitor*. In the following viewpoint, Weisstuch discusses the plans of *Essence*—a black women's magazine—to address the misogyny and sexism present in rap music and current hip-hop culture. She argues that the vulgar lyrics of many songs demean and exploit women. The magazine's campaign attempts to spark dialogue about these vulgar portrayals and to offer a range of perspectives on the topic. The magazine and supporters of the movement recognize that the problem does not apply to all of hip-hop, but they seek to address the forms that do present women in a harmful light.

AS YOU READ, CONSIDER THE FOLLOWING QUESTIONS:
1. How long does the author say that *Essence*'s campaign runs?
2. What music video by rapper Nelly does Weisstuch mention in order to illustrate her argument?
3. As reported in the viewpoint, how do some observers and skeptics view *Essence*'s campaign?

Liza Weisstuch, "Sexism in Rap Sparks Black Magazine to Say, 'Enough!,'" *Christian Science Monitor*, January 12, 2005. Copyright © 2005 by Liza Weisstuch. All rights reserved. Reproduced by permission.

*E*ssence, the black women's magazine, has a daring New Year's resolution: It's embarking on a 12-month campaign to challenge the prevalence of misogyny and sexism in hip-hop lyrics and videos.

Many rappers and MCs[1] coolly objectify women with vulgar song lyrics and hard-hitting, raunchy images on MTV. It's common, for instance, to see videos in which hip-hop artists lounge poolside as a harem of women gyrate around them in bikinis. The video for Nelly's "Tip-Drill" goes so far as to portray scantily clad women as sexual appliances.

The publication's crusade, dubbed Take Back the Music, seeks to inspire public dialogue via magazine features that offer a range of perspectives on the entertainment industry from inside [the industry] as well as [from] outside observers. The January [2005] issue kicks off with comments from artists, critics, and activists.

Monumental Undertaking

Taking on a multibillion-dollar industry that accounts for more music sales than pop and rock—and exerts a cultural influence that extends far beyond the African American community—is a monumental undertaking, even for a publication with a circulation of over 1.6 million. While few expect *Essence* to turn the tide, it's significant that the preeminent magazine for African American women believes that the degree of sexism in rap is no longer tenable.

FAST FACT

According to the *Christian Science Monitor,* many rappers denigrate women with crude song lyrics and vulgar videos.

"This is certainly a women's issue, but it's a black women's issue first," says Michaela Angela Davis, *Essence*'s executive fashion and beauty editor.

"It's fitting that [*Essence* writers] should be the ones to help folks talk about it, listen to each other and have them come up with action steps that make sense to them," she says. "We don't have picket signs,

---

1. Derived from the original abbreviation for "master of ceremonies" (MC); now used as a generic term for a performer who speaks over a beat or performs songs in the hip-hop and rap music genres.

we're not telling people what to think, we're just asking them to think."

The *Essence* campaign is not without precedent. The magazine's staff was galvanized by a much publicized incident at Spelman College in Atlanta last year [2004] in which students at the black women's school protested the appearance of the rapper Nelly for a fundraiser on campus. As part of its campaign, *Essence* will host a "town meeting" at Spelman next month.

"It's a major project in terms of getting young people—white or black—to take these images seriously in a generic culture that exploits and objectifies women," says Beverly Guy-Sheftall, director of the

During a seminar at the Essence *Music Festival in Houston, singer Jill Scott introduces a panel to discuss the role of women and how they are portrayed in music videos. These empowerment seminars were part of the magazine's Take Back the Music campaign.*

Women's Research and Resource Center at Spelman, and co-author of *Gender Talk*.

Last year marked three decades since hip-hop emerged on the streets of New York. Since then, it's established itself at the vanguard of pop culture. As an influence on fashion and other genres of music, hip-hop has had a colossal impact. But hip-hop culture hasn't always been as sexist as it is now.

Ms. Davis, also a founding editor of *Vibe* [magazine], notes that hip-hop has "gone through a funnel." It started off broadly, encompassing a variety of genres, and progressed from the political to the more avant-garde and satirical.

But as "gangsta rap" has come to the fore, so have lyrics that glorify violence and misogyny.

Hip-Hop Is Not the First
Of course, hip-hop is hardly the first, or only, form of contemporary music to portray women in an unflattering light. In the 1970s, and even

"All right! You win! — there *is* something worse than Gangsta Rap!"

"All right! You win!—there *is* something worse than Gangsta Rap!," cartoon by Baloo-Rex May. www.Cartoon Stock.com.

more so in the 1980s, it was the spandex-clad, heavy metal crowd whose lyrics, videos, and album covers portrayed women as sexual objects.

That certainly suggests that the demeaning of women—and even misogyny—is a part of a wider societal problem that isn't peculiar to hip-hop. Nor is it just a black problem, since white consumers account for a huge share of hip-hop sales.

Some observers, however, see *Essence*'s campaign as another attempt to lash out at hip-hop's free, and at times subversive, expression.

"If anyone singles out hip-hop, that's unfortunate: Hip-hop started in mid '70s, and sexism and misogyny have been around much longer," says Dr. Todd Boyd, author of numerous books on African American pop culture and a professor of critical studies at the School of Cinema-Television at the University of Southern California in Los Angeles.

"It's one thing to challenge cultural representations in society at large—in hip-hop, television, movies—but to single out hip-hop is another example of people criticizing hip-hop without knowing much about it," he says. "It points to people's dislike of hip-hop but doesn't do much to advance whatever issue they have."

But Dr. Guy-Sheftall of Spelman College says that *Essence*'s campaign is a nuanced one that recognizes that not all hip-hop is problematic.

Nobody involved in the campaign is under the illusion that taking on a pop-culture powerhouse will be easy, but they're hoping that diverse forms of hip-hop—less exploitative of women—will nudge aside the more objectionable content that dominates the Top 40 airwaves.

"[But] we don't see diversity coming on its own without action taken by individuals," says Davis. "It'd be wonderful if [society could] have a more accurate view of who [African American women] really are."

EVALUATING THE AUTHOR'S ARGUMENTS:

What would Liza Weisstuch say to Bakari Kitwana's argument in the previous viewpoint—that hip-hop activism can be used to fight domestic violence? Whose position do you find more convincing, Weisstuch's or Kitwana's? Explain your answers using evidence from the viewpoints.

Viewpoint 2

Rap Music Has a Long Tradition of Feminism

Akoto Ofori-Atta

"Hip-hop feminists are like other feminists in that they advocate for gender equality."

Akoto Ofori-Atta is the assistant editor of the *Root*. In the following viewpoint, she argues that hip-hop has long had a feminist tradition. She says that hip-hop feminists advocate gender equality and also identify as part of hip-hop culture and activism. Hip-hop feminism needs to do more than simply push back against misogynistic lyrics that express hatred toward women, argues Ofori-Atta. She says it should also create a positive vision for young women who want both to be treated equally and to express their sexuality. She concludes that both women and men need to be involved in creating a hip-hop feminism.

AS YOU READ, CONSIDER THE FOLLOWING QUESTIONS:

1. According to Ofori-Atta, how did Don Imus justify his misogynistic comments about black women?
2. The hip-hop generation was born between what years, according to the author?
3. Who is Nicki Minaj, and how does Ofori-Atta say she challenges stereotypes about female rappers?

Akoto Ofori-Atta, "Is Hip-Hop Feminism Alive in 2011?," *Root*, March 21, 2011. www.theroot.com.

In 1992 [rapper] Dr. Dre released his single "Bitches Ain't Sh--," complete with a chorus that emphatically reduces women to nothing but "hoes and tricks." In 1996 [rapper] Akinyele famously sang "Put It In Your Mouth," a song that flooded radio airwaves and clubs across the country.

Hip-Hop Feminism

Fast-forward to 2003, and [hip-hop artist] Nelly releases a video for his single "Tip Drill," in which he famously slides a credit card between the cheeks of a video vixen's bottom. And then there was, of course, the [talk-radio host] Don Imus incident, when he justified his "nappy-headed ho" comment [in 2007] by arguing that black men regularly call their women out of their names in hip-hop songs.

There is no shortage of these cringe-inducing moments that have made women question their relationship to hip-hop. But these moments don't go completely uncontested. From Queen Latifah's "U.N.I.T.Y." ("Who you callin' a bitch?") to a 10-year-old's heartfelt plea to Lil Wayne urging him to speak highly of women, hip-hop feminism has almost always been just as audible as the crass catcalls. While one might be hard-pressed to find a song of the "Put It In Your Mouth" variety in heavy rotation today, hip-hop feminists still have a job to do in railing against a male-dominated culture.

Hip-hop feminists are like other feminists in that they advocate for gender equality. Where they part ways from other feminist groups is that they operate in and identify as part of hip-hop culture, as expressed in their choices in music, dance, art and politics.

Leaving Behind Rap's Misogyny

For some, the term "hip-hop feminism" offers up quite the enigma. Critics position misogyny as hip-hop's cardinal sin, which raises the obvious question: How do women actively participate in a culture that seems to hate them so vehemently? For self-described hip-hop feminists, attempting to answer that question is not their only task, since understanding what hip-hop feminism is and isn't goes far beyond responding to women-bashing sentiment.

"I could care less about what these boys are expressing in their lyrics, whether it's misogynistic or sexist or not, because we've had that conversation," says Joan Morgan, author of the seminal book *When Chickenheads Come Home to Roost: My Life as a Hip-Hop Feminist.* Today's hip-hop feminists, she says, should be focused on addressing other critical issues, like challenging the "respectability politics" that keep black women from freely expressing their sexuality.

Morgan did not coin the term "hip-hop feminist" until 1999, but rap's pro-woman consciousness dates back further, with artists like Queen Latifah, MC Lyte, Tupac and Eve making music with a distinctly feminist sensibility. But promoting and recognizing artists and lyrics that support women in hip-hop is only part of hip-hop feminism's agenda.

Fast Fact

The first female rap solo artist to record was Philadelphia-based Lady B, who released "To the Beat Y'all" on Sugar Hill Records in 1980.

"I was never talking about tracks made by female artists," Morgan says of her book, which was the first to articulate the dichotomy of hip-hop feminism. "I was talking about hip-hop culture, and the ways that people move through it. I don't think a hip-hop feminist critique can do the work it needs to do if it can't analyze all of it."

Black Feminism Versus Hip-Hop Feminism

To be certain, hip-hop feminism was born out of a need to understand the many cultural, social and political conditions that afflicted women of what Bakari Kitwana called the hip-hop generation, comprised of people born between 1965 and 1985. Black feminism, a wave of thought and activism largely influenced by the civil rights and black power movements, was not equipped to consider the issues of women belonging to the hip-hop generation.

Hip-hop's babies weren't dealing directly with issues of invisibility brought on by systems of segregation the way the generations were that came before them. Instead, they were grappling with being front and center as the most loved and most hated stars of global popular culture. The popularity of hip-hop made black youth cool and desirable, which was in complete opposition to the unavoidable stereotypes in the media that illustrated them as gang members, welfare queens, drug dealers and teen mothers.

"The manifestos of black feminism, while they helped me to understand the importance of articulating language to combat oppression, didn't give me the language to explore things that were not black and white, but things that were in the gray," Morgan says. "And that gray is very much represented in hip-hop."

This gray area includes the contradictions of loving an art that is reluctant to include you; loving men who, at times, refuse to portray you in your totality; and rejecting sexual objectification while actively and proudly embracing your sexuality. Although hip-hop feminism has gone through phases, it has always, at some level, dealt with these incongruities.

"Hip-hop feminists have been consistent in championing women's rights, which encompasses everything from sexuality to abuse," says

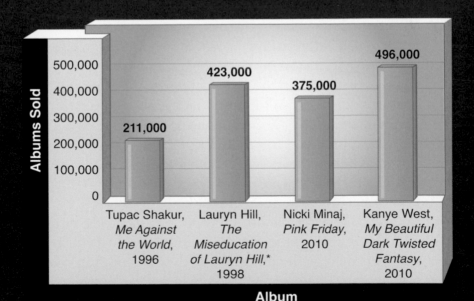

First Week Album Sales for Selected Hip-Hop Artists

*Highest number of first week sales to date for a female hip-hop artist.

Taken from: The YBF, "Nicki Minaj's Album Sales Make History + Maino Arrested!," December 10, 2010. http://theybf.com
and Jerry Crowe, "All Eyes on Shakur's 'Don Killuminati,'" Los Angeles Times, November 14, 1996. www.latimes.co

Marcyliena Morgan, founding director of the Hip-Hop Archive in the W.E.B. Du Bois Institute at Harvard University. "And that has always been irrespective of what men in hip-hop were doing."

What the Future Holds

So what should hip-hop feminism look like in 2011? Instead of being reduced to an anti-misogyny movement or to a rallying cry to give more female MCs[1] the mic, hip-hop feminists hope that it will incorporate a women-centric worldview, where the realities of the hip-hop generation's women are taken into consideration at every turn. It doesn't just complain about the lack of female MCs but actively addresses the reasons there are fewer female MCs now than there were in the late 1980s, and why there are only a few types of female MCs that make it to hip-hop notoriety.

Joan Morgan also thinks that hip-hop feminism needs to evolve so that it can address the curious case of hip-hop's most current and colorful female character, Nicki Minaj. Minaj may be the most visible example of female resistance from an artist. Whether she is professing, as she did on Kanye West's song "Monster," "You could be the king, but watch the queen conquer," or being open about her bi-curiosity, Minaj embraces female power and challenges norms of sexuality that black female hip-hop artists have not always embraced.

"We don't even know what to make of her, and we don't even know if she's straight or not," Morgan says. "I want to see the creation of language that pushes us to have a more in-depth conversation about Nikki Minaj, that doesn't just compare her to Lil' Kim, because she is not Lil' Kim."

And perhaps Minaj doesn't know what to make of herself. As she once told an interviewer, "[W]hen I grew up I saw females doing certain things, and I thought I had to do that exactly. The female rappers of my day spoke about sex a lot . . . and I thought that to have the success they got, I would have to represent the same thing, when in fact I didn't have to represent the same thing."

For up-and-coming female MCs, the opportunity to be recognized as Grade A performers who can co-exist and share stages with Grade A male rappers may be the difference between a hip-hop feminism that works and one that doesn't. Nicki Lynette, a Chicago-based art-

1. Derived from the original abbreviation for "master of ceremonies" (MC); now used as a generic term for a performer who speaks over a beat or performs songs in the hip-hop and rap music genres.

Rapper Nicki Minaj (pictured) is well known for challenging the norms of sexuality that black female hip-hop artists have been reluctant to embrace.

ist whose music blends hip-hop, funk and pop, says that she didn't realize she held feminist views until she was asked to do an all-female showcase and mixtape.

"I said no because I think it's anti-feminist to make women in hip-hop a sideshow," Lynette told the *Root* [magazine]. "A show that includes several hot MCs, both male and female, and is less concerned about making the distinction between men and women makes more sense to me."

But perhaps hip-hop feminism's most important task is staying keenly attuned to the needs of the hip-hop community. Hip-hop feminism, just like any branch of feminism, should use activism to effect real social change. This requires all members of the hip-hop generation to get on board.

So it's not just women who are tasked with tapping into the creative resources that give hip-hop's women a voice. "[Duke University professor] Mark Anthony Neal's work [on gender and feminism] is a good example of this," says Marcyliena Morgan [a professor of African and African American Studies at Harvard University]. "The one thing that hip-hop feminism has taught anyone is that feminism must include the efforts of the entire community, men and women alike."

EVALUATING THE AUTHOR'S ARGUMENTS:

Akoto Ofori-Atta quotes rapper Nicki Lynette saying that an all-female mixtape would make women a sideshow and that she would rather produce a tape with rappers of both sexes. Would a mixtape featuring all men make men a sideshow? Why or why not? Does Lynette's stance seem consistent with Ofori-Atta's belief that hip-hop feminism should focus on Nicki Minaj? Explain your answer.

Men and Women Should Reject Misogynistic Rap

"Distancing ourselves from commercial rap with no commitment to women's progress might be temporarily necessary."

Liz Funk

Liz Funk is an author, blogger, and speaker whose work has appeared in *USA Today*, *Newsday*, the *Washington Post*, and numerous other publications. In the following viewpoint, she argues that hip-hop is an artistic movement for progressive change rooted in oppression. She says that rap, on the other hand, is commercial music. Funk argues that progressives need to explain the difference between hip-hop and rap. She says they need to be willing to condemn misogyny—or hatred toward women—in rap and to explain that such misogyny is not in keeping with hip-hop's traditions.

AS YOU READ, CONSIDER THE FOLLOWING QUESTIONS:

1. According to Funk, why have many women not expressed outrage at misogynistic rap lyrics?
2. What does the author say *Essence* magazine did in response to misogyny in rap?
3. What evidence from a 2003 study does Funk cite to show that rap misogyny can damage women?

"**S** mack that, all on the floor. Smack that, give me some more. Smack that, 'till you get sore." —Akon, "Smack That." . . .

This is a benign sampling of the lyrics from popular misogynistic hip-hop and rap songs today. The music industry has openly embraced the lucrative aspects of these sexist tunes, and surprisingly, women haven't expressed outrage.

Female Chauvinist Pigs

Why? Because many women love these songs. Several prominent contemporary feminists and feminist writers, most notably, Ariel Levy, have identified a trend within American society of women espousing and feeling empowered by enterprises and activities that many feminists feel have historically oppressed women. Levy discussed this trend in her October 2005 book *Female Chauvinist Pigs: Women and the Rise of Raunch Culture.*

"[Sexist lyrics] usually come to a good beat. I like to bump and grind to it," says Natasha Miner, a college student from New York City, in a *WireTap* interview. "I don't care if it's sexist music at a club. . . . I don't think girls are looking for their music to be 'empowering,' or whatever, but then again, I don't think people really care to consider that stuff."

Filmmaker and anti-sexist hip-hop activist Byron Hurt tackles this issue in his newest film, *Hip-Hop: Beyond Beats and Rhymes.* Hurt is a devoted feminist who has made a long career of meeting men where they are at, but pushing a strong message of anti-sexism and anti-violence. He founded Mentors in Violence Prevention, a rape and domestic violence prevention program for professional athletes, and served as the associate director of the United States Marine Corps' first gender violence prevention program.

"I guess what I'm trying to do is to get us men to take a hard look at ourselves," Hurt says in the first scene of the film. He describes manhood as, "Like, we're in this box, and in order to be in that box you have to be strong, tough, you have to have a lot of girls, you gotta have money, you have to be a player or a pimp, you have to be in control, you have to dominate other men, other people, other men. And if you're not any of those things, people will call you soft, weak, a p*ssy, chump, faggot and no one wants to be any of those things, so

Antisexism hip-hop activist and filmmaker Byron Hurt (pictured) has been promoting a strong message of antisexism and antiviolence to the hip-hop community. He founded Mentors in Violence Prevention, a rape and domestic violence prevention program.

they stay inside the box." Hurt articulates the state of contemporary rap and hip-hop and offers hope for lovers of the "beats and rhymes" . . . while others feel that demystifying the controversy inherent in hip-hop will guide it back to its original purpose.

Hip-Hop and the Mainstream

A blogger for Young People For's blog wrote in a recent post called "Blame hip-hop for society's ills, but what of its successes?":

> With the idea that we now live on a Hip-hop Planet comes the problem with commercially motivated and corporately owned hip-hop and its detriment on society. Today's *New York Times* has an article titled "Don't Blame Hip-Hop," speaking how one cannot blame hip-hop for culture's ills, but rather the corporation. [Talk-show host Don] Imus blamed hip-hop and Oprah blames hip-hop for problems in society, and they are within their rights because [they feel hip-hop stirs unneeded controversy]. Now in all other cases, especially the case of hip-hop, controversy is the

purpose, but this controversy is about the missed purpose. Hip-hop is rooted in oppression, race and class. What the movement has become now is questionable. "We were about the movement," Abiodun Oyewole, a founder of the Last Poets, says. "A lot of today's rappers have talent. But a lot of them are driving the car in the wrong direction."

This blogger distinguishes that hip-hop is "rooted in oppression, race and class." However, Natasha doesn't know the difference between rap and hip-hop (and truth be told, few who aren't involved with hip-hop do). Hip-hop, as discussed above, is historically associated with social change and ameliorating society's issues, whereas rap is a commercially driven trade. So the question of whether rap artists are bound to feminist traditions arises. But then again, is there really any excuse for misogyny? Can exalting misogyny for commercial gain ever be condoned by the progressive community? No.

Other activists have sought solutions for the problem, including the staffers of *Essence* magazine, who launched the Take Back the Music campaign in January of 2005 to examine the negative portrayal of women of color in rap and hip-hop and propose solutions to said problem. Their mission statement explains, "We at *Essence* have become increasingly concerned about the degrading ways in which black women are portrayed and spoken about in popular media, particularly in popular urban music and music videos. Aware that these images may be having a negative impact on our children, we realized that, as black women, it was up to us to take a stand."

FAST FACT

One study among university students found that those who listened to heavy metal expressed more hostile attitudes toward women than did those who listened to rap.

Misogynistic Rap Is Damaging

Studies even support arguments that misogynistic rap and hip-hop is clearly damaging: a 2003 Emory study showed that African American young women from rural Alabama between the ages of 14 and 18,

All-Time Top Rap Album Sales as of 2011

Rankings: Album Sales	
Artist	**Total Sales**
1. Eminem	**7,516,000**
2. Lil Wayne	2,978,000
3. Jay-Z	2,746,000
4. Kanye West	2,158,000
5. Drake	2,037,000
6. T.I.	1,558,000
7. Nicki Minaj	1,500,000
8. Rick Ross	1,257,000
9. Kid Cudi	1,069,000
10. Gucci Mane	1,017,000
11. Ludacris	967,000
12. Snoop Dogg	734,000
13. Wiz Khalifa	639,000
14. Lupe Fiasco	579,000
15. B.O.B.	568,000
16. Pitbull	480,000
17. Fabolous	441,000
18. Diddy	301,000
19. Waka Flocka Flame	285,000
20. Big Boi	230,000

Taken from: Chris Molanphy, "Introducing the King of Hip-Hop," *Rolling Stone*, August 15, 2011. www.rollingstone.com.

who watched more than 14 hours of misogynistic rap and hip-hop were more likely to engage in "risky" behavior.

[African American activist] Al Sharpton has even weighed in on the issue: "If they've got the right to call my daughter a b----, I have a right to say 'boycott.'" While few progressives advocate for the censorship of rap and hip-hop, pro-hip-hop progressives owe it to the history of hip-hop to advocate against the inequality and manifest hypocrisy inherent in misogynistic hip-hop.

An ideal step to take is to, first and foremost, articulate the differences between rap and hip-hop to the mainstream populace and casual listeners, and explain how hip-hop is a means of social change; distancing ourselves from commercial rap with no commitment to women's progress might be temporarily necessary. While some progressive politicians are willing to distance themselves from women's progress, it is the duty of the progressive movement to voice its distaste for misogyny and reclaim hip-hop. Hip-hop is great music (as is a lot of rap) . . . however, it can be even better when it empowers all involved parties.

EVALUATING THE AUTHOR'S ARGUMENTS:

Based on Liz Funk's discussion, what music or culture discussed by Brian Sims, Bakari Kitwana, or Akoto Ofori-Atta—authors of three previous viewpoints—would be considered hip-hop? What music or culture discussed by these three authors would be considered rap?

Hip-Hop Prison Culture Hurts Women

"Songs perpetuate the idea that in order to exhibit true devotion, girls must put up with all manner of negative and detrimental behavior."

Prison Culture

Prison Culture is a blog devoted to the subjects of mass incarceration and the American prison system. In the following viewpoint, the author argues that many rap songs by men and women alike focus on men going to prison. In these songs, the author points out, women are expected to wait loyally for men to return. In some cases the women are also expected to take over the men's criminal enterprises. The author argues that women should not feel they have to wait for their men and should not be encouraged to engage in criminal behavior as proof of their love. The author concludes that these images of loyal women and imprisoned men may hurt women.

AS YOU READ, CONSIDER THE FOLLOWING QUESTIONS:
1. What are the chances that white, black, and Latino males have of serving time in prison, according to the viewpoint?
2. What does the viewpoint say embodies true love and devotion in Da Bart's "Ghetto Love"?
3. As reported in the viewpoint, how did T.I.'s incarceration differ from that of many young men who go to prison?

For the last few years, I have observed a prevalence of images of prison in rap and r & b songs and videos. Certainly this trend mirrors reality because so many men of color (and increasingly black women) find themselves implicated in the criminal legal system. In fact, one in ten black males aged 25–29 was in prison or jail in 2009 as were 1 in 25 Latino males in the same age group. Black males have a 32% chance of serving time in prison at some point in their lives; Latino males have a 17% chance; while white males have only a 6% chance (Bureau of Justice Statistics). Nearly one in three (32%) black males in the age group 20–29 is under some form of criminal justice supervision on any given day—either in prison or jail, or on probation or parole.

Women, Men, and Prison

Some popular past hip hop videos such as Alicia Keys's "Fallin'" and Eve's "Gotta Man" show women dutifully supporting men who are incarcerated. The performers longingly sing about the day when their partners will be released from the pen.

One classic illustration of the "prison love" theme from a female perspective is Da Brat's song "Ghetto Love" from her album "Anuthatantrum" (1996).

The following is a key excerpt from the song:

. . . Taught me how to measure grams, cook rocks, and chop weights.

Caught a case 'cause your boy ran his mouth too much . . .

But they can keep pacin' 'cause I'm gonna be waitin' on my baby. . . .

These lyrics illustrate Da Brat's initiation into a life of drug dealing and her boyfriend's subsequent arrest and incarceration. She takes over the business while he is away, all the while waiting for his eventual release. This is supposed to embody true love and devotion. While this may indeed be the reality for some young women, this and other songs perpetuate the idea that in order to exhibit true devotion, girls must put up with all manner of negative and detrimental behavior. This notion is also articulated by male performers.

For instance in his song "21 Questions," 50 cent asks:

. . . If I got locked up and sentenced to a quarter century

could I count on you to be there to support me mentally? . . .

The video for the song picks up on the "prison" theme and expands upon it. We watch as 50 cent is talking to the beautiful [actress] Zoe Saldana from jail. In another scene, she is helping him to hide a stack of money as the cops move in to apparently make an arrest. The

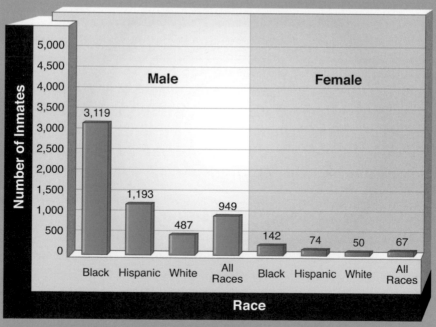

Number of Incarcerated Persons per 100,000 Population, 2009

Taken from: Family Facts, "African-American Males Are More Likely than Others to Be Incarcerated," FamilyFacts.org.
Source: Bureau of Justice Statistics, 2010.

In 2010 Rapper T.I. married Tameka "Tiny" Cottle after she had stood by him during his prison incarceration.

unequivocal message is that black women need to prove their loyalty to their "men" by putting themselves at risk of incarceration by participating in criminal activity or aiding and abetting said man. These girls are implicated in the crime either because they actively take part in it or because they harbor the person who is committing the crime.

Stand by Your Locked-Up Man

[Scholars Johnetta Betsch] Cole and [Beverly] Guy-Sheftall (2003) correctly assert that "the women many hip-hop songs celebrate are valued primarily for satisfying their men sexually and providing whatever support they need. Tragically, many young women even pass the ultimate test of loyalty by endangering themselves and their futures, including the risk of incarceration, through drug use, burglary, or prostitution, all in the name of 'love.'"

So this brings me to the most recent example of a "stand by your locked up man" rap song. The popular rapper T.I recently [on July 30, 2010] married his long time girlfriend Tiny [Cottle] after having served a one year prison sentence. He has talked very lovingly about the fact that she stood by him while he was in prison. While this is great for Tiny as this was her choice, I don't want the message going out to young black women that they have to spend years "waiting" for men they love to get out of prison for the promise of marriage. T.I. served less than a year in prison and he is a rich rapper. Many young men who are locked up are unfortunately there for much longer sentences and also do not come out to a successful entertainment career. The stresses imposed on young women whose partners are incarcerated are incalculable and I really feel queasy that the message in hip hop is that they are expected to patiently wait for incarcerated men to return or worse yet to pick up their criminal enterprises while they are on the inside.

To be fair, T.I's "Got Your Back" is really more of a love letter to his wife rather than an encouragement to engage in a life of crime. However it seems important to highlight the issues raised by this and other songs that feature women being expected to have their partners' backs while they are incarcerated. These are not uncomplicated decisions. I want young women to find happiness in their lives and if they make a choice to wait because this is a clear headed decision, then great. However, if they are making the choice because of social pressure and the weight of expectations, then this is necessarily destructive.

EVALUATING THE AUTHOR'S ARGUMENTS:

According to this viewpoint, why is loyalty to men, especially while they are in prison, a key theme in rap songs? What different explanation is presented by Brian Sims in viewpoint 5 of chapter 1? Which explanation seems more convincing, and why?

R&B Is More Harmful to Women than Rap

Brandon Soderberg

"Then there's the disturbing trend over the past decade for R&B seduction songs to hinge on booze consumption, turning much of the genre into a series of date-rape ballads."

Brandon Soderberg has written for *Spin*, the *Village Voice*, *Pitchfork*, and numerous other outlets. In the following viewpoint, he argues that rhythm and blues (R&B) music has become increasingly misogynistic, or characterized by hatred toward women. Soderberg says that R&B men often sing about abuse or about drugging women into unconsciousness in order to rape them. On the other hand, he argues, rap has become more mature and focused on adult relationships. He concludes that R&B today is often more immature and more misogynistic than rap.

1. According to Soderberg, after which incidents was Chris Brown labeled a rapper?
2. How does the author describe the Weeknd?
3. In Soderberg's view, why is R&B's brand of sexual violence more realistic than rap's?

Rap and R&B right now are, for the most part, interchangeable. That's not a complaint, it's a simple fact of contemporary urban music. R&B grabbed some of rap's edginess so it didn't become mom-and-girlfriend music, and rap successfully teamed up with R&B to create what [American hip-hop trio] De La Soul once called "rap and bullshit." But even though rap's still up for criticism by any and everyone (even Ashley Judd! [an actress who criticized rap's misogyny in her 2011 memoir]), it's rare to hear serious complaints about the content of the latest slow jam. If rap has to deal with all of R&B's corny nonsense, then R&B should have to deal with some of the fallout from those who still claim rap is corrupting America.

Confusing Rap and R&B

A fun game is spotting the random African American male crooner who gets tagged as a "rapper" by any number of clueless newspapers or magazines. There's an implicit value judgment made when, say, Ne-Yo receives the "rapper" label: This stuff, with its futuristic synths and bold drums and sexually explicit lyrics, is *not* R&B (a.k.a., love songs for grown-ass men and women). Even more common is the act of referring to a troubled R&B singer as a "rapper." Google "rapper R. Kelly" and see what comes up. Chris Brown was suddenly a "rapper" around the time he viciously assaulted Rihanna [his girlfriend in 2009] and, once again, when he threw a chair at a window after he was asked about Rihanna in an interview with journalistic heavy-hitters *Good Morning America* [in 2011].

Brown, ever the opportunistic shitbag in his post-Rihanna career, has welcomed and even exploited the rapper tag. It's a minor but not insignificant part of why he's been able to make such a bold comeback. His song "Deuces" received an epic rap remix, and America's favorite young domestic abuser even rhymes alongside Busta Rhymes and Lil Wayne on America's current [April 2011] No. 1 R&B/Hip-Hop single "Look At Me Now." By rapping a bit, even dying his hair blonde, or possibly leaking that nude photo of himself, Brown conveys some vague sense of danger and suggests a hip-hop reinvention that distracts from, or at least recasts, his controversy: No longer was he the sweet young R&B singer who beat up Rihanna, he was now the impervious *rapper* who beat up Rihanna. Ultimately, Brown copped-out on the rapper schtick. *F.A.M.E.* (which stands for "Forgiving All My Enemies") is essentially an R&B album full of gross horny crooner tracks and Euro-trashy party pumpers. Still, this is a pretty fascinating phenomenon: The girlfriend-beating R&B loverman dabbles in hip-hop to *improve* his public image.

The Offensive Aspects of R&B

R&B's lewd self-parody is bad enough (from *F.A.M.E.*'s "No Bullshit"): "Three in the morning / You know I'm horny / So why don't you come over my place / Put a smile on my face?" Then there's the disturbing trend over the past decade for R&B seduction songs to hinge on booze consumption, turning much of the genre into a series of date-rape ballads. Jamie Foxx's loathsome "Blame It on the Alcohol" is the blueprint.

As a result, R&B actually has become much more offensive than rap. Mysterious Toronto group the Weeknd have made a name for themselves recently by focusing on the ickier aspects of R&B. Their mixtape, *House Of Balloons*, is a nine-song collection of stretched-out electronic grooves that's just a bit more ominous than what's on the radio at the moment; content-wise, though, *House Of Balloons* seems intent on taking the models-and-bottles, all-night-party creepiness of radio R&B to new levels. "High For This" walks a partner through a

Oscar-winning actor and musician Jamie Foxx has come under fire for his song "Blame It on the Alcohol," which critics say is a prime example of a date-rape ballad.

dangerous escapade, while warning her that she'll "want to be high for this." . . .

Maybe these Canadians are conducting some sort of deconstructionist project, trying to bring shame back to the game, but their mixtape is proudly dark and nihilistic. This couplet from "Wicked Games" is, like most of the album, sung with a smirk: "Bring your love, baby / I can bring my shame / Bring the drugs, baby / I can bring my pain." The group's lightning-fast hype and strangely on-the-mark "indie" approach to mainstream R&B has left many suspicious. Whether it's cool or totally bullshit to dig them is a pretty boring debate. But when the same people who are up-in-arms about [rap group] Odd Future's rape-referencing raps gloss over the Weeknd's lyrics—which are mostly about drinking with, or drugging, women past the point of consciousness—that's particularly fascinating.

The controversy over Odd Future actually has a lot to do with how rare the group's type of dark humor has become within hip-hop, and illustrates just how tame the genre is right now by comparison, espe-

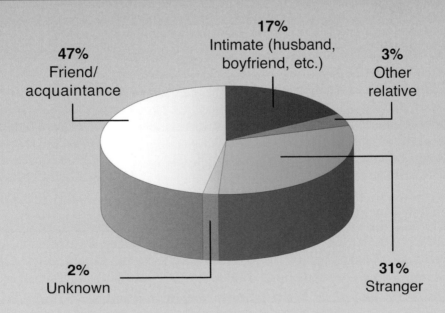

Relationships Between Sexually Assaulted Women and Their Attackers, 2004

The chart below shows the relationship between the perpetrators of rape or other sexual assaults and the women aged twelve and older who are their victims.

47%
Friend/
acquaintance

17%
Intimate (husband,
boyfriend, etc.)

3%
Other
relative

2%
Unknown

31%
Stranger

Taken from: US Department of Health and Human Services, Health Resources and Services Administration, Maternal and Child Health Bureau, *Women's Health, USA 2006*. Rockville, MD: US Department of Health and Human Services, 2006.

cially when you focus on R&B's drug-and-alcohol-fueled scenarios. Plus, the Weeknd's brand of sexual violation is far closer to real life than Tyler, the Creator's Ted Bundy fantasies.[1] When critics and commenters scrutinize the latter and not the former, we help create or reaffirm simplistic notions of what rape actually is, and how it occurs. Rarely is the rapist a stranger in an alley wearing a ski mask. He's the mildly charming douche handing you drinks all night.

Worse than Rap

A scan through R&B radio for something a bit less nefarious leaves one with very few options. Indeed, some of the only bona fide love songs these days are rap-informed R&B or just straight-up hip-hop. . . .

[Rapper] Fabolous' "You Be Killin' Em" is a clever twist on New York punch-line rap, with Fab employing his talent for turns of phrase to praise a female ("Louis Vuitton shoes, she got too much pride / Her feet are killin' her / I call it shoe-a-cide"). A recently announced sequel to the song features R&B nice guys Ne-Yo and Ryan Leslie. Late last week, Jay-Z appeared on a remix of Sade's "Moon & the Stars" for an upcoming greatest-hits collection, and though his verse is one of Jay's do-this-for-the-culture type deals, it is nonetheless a mature look into post-break-up mistakes. And that's more than you can say for most contemporary R&B singers.

Kanye West's "All Of The Lights," meanwhile, is an empathetic, though still devastating, portrayal of an abusive husband suffering the consequences of his actions. "I slapped my girl, she called the Feds," he whines in the first verse; afterwards, he's saddled with a restraining order and public visitations with his kids. It's a song about consequences. Rihanna sings the hook.

And there was Rihanna last year [2010] on Eminem's pop smash "Love The Way You Lie," another abuse slow-burner. Perhaps the obvious problem is really just the state of R&B's men? Though in the end, Em rapping "I'm a liar / If she ever f---in' tries to leave again / I'ma tie her to the bed / And set this house on fire" isn't exactly a step forward, it does feel like an honest attempt to describe the dangerous

---

1. Tyler, the Creator, is a rapper in the group Odd Future. Ted Bundy was a serial killer in the 1970s, who was executed for his crimes in 1989.

arc of co-dependence and doesn't sugarcoat or sidestep issues of abuse. Chris Brown and, well, much of the R&B world should listen and take notes. Much the same way R&B regained some measure of realness and callow fun by co-opting hip-hop, it seems that now, ironically, it could regain some of its maturity from rap as well.

EVALUATING THE AUTHOR'S ARGUMENTS:

In arguing that R&B is misogynistic, Brandon Soderberg focuses on male performers. If female performers (like Rihanna or Sade, both of whom Soderberg mentions) were included, would R&B seem less misogynistic? Explain your reasoning.

Viewpoint
6

R&B Can Teach Feminist Lessons

Sarah Jaffe

Sarah Jaffe is an associate editor at AlterNet; her writing has also appeared in the *Nation*, the *American Prospect*, *Bust*, and other publications. In the following viewpoint, she praises the music she grew up with in the 1980s and 1990s for its pro-feminist message. Jaffe says that artists like Salt-n-Pepa, En Vogue, and Janet Jackson taught her to be independent and to take control of her life and her sexuality. She suggests that those kinds of positive messages, delivered by newer artists like Beyoncé and Nicki Minaj, are still on the radio for young girls.

"The messages culture sends you seep in best when you're young."

AS YOU READ, CONSIDER THE FOLLOWING QUESTIONS:
1. Why does Jaffe say that Salt-n-Pepa's "Shoop" was an important song for her?
2. How did Janet Jackson's aesthetic from her *Rhythm Nation* tour shape the way Jaffe dresses?
3. Why does the author say she loves Beyoncé's latest album?

Sarah Jaffe, "Control: Or, How I Learned My Feminism From 80's and 90's Women in R&B," *Feministe* (blog), August 15, 2011. www.feministe.us/blog. Copyright © 2011 by Sarah Jaffe. All rights reserved. Reproduced by permission.

W ell before I was even remotely cool enough to listen to music that wasn't on the radio, I was surrounded by a fierce pro-woman message. . . .

"Let's Talk About Sex"

Salt-n-Pepa [female rap group] talked about talking about sex in all its particulars and then kept doing it; "Shoop" [1993] was the earliest song about female desire that I knew all the words to, and I remember singing it along with girlfriends in grade school as we talked about our crushes. And then they reminded us that we didn't have to talk about sex if we didn't want to, either [in the song "Let's Talk About Sex," 1992]:

> "How many rules am I to break before you understand
> That your double-standards don't mean shit to me?"

En Vogue! "Never Gonna Get It" [that is, "My Lovin' (You're Never Gonna Get It)," from 1992] echoed in my head; it wasn't just saying "No," it was glorying in the ability to choose. And "Free Your Mind," [1992] like "Let's Talk About Sex" was pretty clearly political.

FAST FACT

Janet Jackson's 1993 album *janet* sold more than 7 million copies. The single "That's the Way Love Goes" topped the Hot 100 charts for eight straight weeks.

And we can't for a minute forget [musical trio] TLC, right? I went on a binge of all this music earlier this summer, and it occurred to me that Left Eye [a rapper in TLC] was actually the precursor to Nicki Minaj [a female rapper who became popular beginning in 2007], her flow and her voice, her blend of attitude and cartoonish girl-voice, daring you to not take her seriously. But it wasn't just Lisa [Left Eye] Lopes, who died on my birthday back in 2002; it was all of them, it was their songs, their utter domination of the charts, their reiteration over and over that we didn't need the boys who made us feel so damn unpretty, that they didn't want no scrubs—but more importantly, that they had each others' backs.

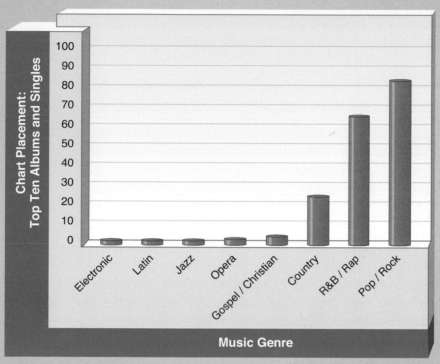

America's Music Genre Preferences, 2008

Chart Placement: Top Ten Albums and Singles

Music Genre

Electronic — Latin — Jazz — Opera — Gospel / Christian — Country — R&B / Rap — Pop / Rock

Taken from: Randall Robert, "Hitsville: The Year in Music, by the Numbers, *LA Weekly Blogs*, December 17, 2008. http://blogs.laweekly.com.

We went from these groups to Britney Spears and Christina Aguilera [pop stars popular beginning in the mid- and late 1990s]; from coalitions of women together to solo whitegirl [sic] pop stars, and I'm not trying to say anyone's wrong for liking their music, but think about the message that we had when three women of color sat together atop the Billboard charts, and what that message was traded for when we got Britney in her schoolgirl skirt instead.

Janet Jackson

But hell, before any of these groups made it to my consciousness, there was Janet.

I really rediscovered Janet Jackson this year thanks to Rachel [La Bruyere, an organizer and blogger] and Megan [Carpentier, executive editor of *Raw Story*, an online news site], first Rachel's suggestion of plugging Janet into Pandora (or in my case Last.fm) [two music listening sites that recommend songs] and enjoying the results, and then burning *Rhythm Nation 1814* [Jackson's fourth album, released in 1989] onto my iPod at Megan's over some delicious peach daiquiris. And how the heck had I let her lapse so long? It's not like she went away, oh no. From the time I saw her play, my second concert ever, age 10, with my babysitter (my mother was more of a Neil Diamond fan), I had posters of Janet on my walls; from the time I heard "Control," probably with another babysitter, I'd been a fan. And she's been making music as long as I've been alive.

Control [1986] is a classic, a record made by a young woman asserting herself and her beliefs. "What Have You Done For Me Lately" is as great a pop song about a lousy boyfriend as has been written, and "Nasty" was my theme song when I was far too young to know what it meant—I remember doing a dance performance to it in summer camp. And she spoke up for "The Pleasure Principle" early on even when also insisting on her right to say "Let's Wait Awhile."

Rhythm Nation was Janet's step toward politics, but even that record is full of pure-bliss dance tracks like "Miss You Much," "Alright," and "Escapade." Just try not to shake it to any of those songs. I dare you. And "Black Cat" prefigured my love for hard rock. Hell, Janet's aesthetic from that tour probably shaped the way I've dressed for the rest of my life: skinny black pants, military jackets, big boots.

But, . . . none of those songs were the ones that were really revolutionary for me.

No, that was "If."

"If"

I remember when it dropped, when MTV had a huge "WORLD PREMIERE" tag and it was 1993 and I was beginning to suspect that radio pop wasn't the only thing out there for an angry teenage girl.

But. "If." She sang *if I was your girl the things I'd do to you*, and then she went on to name them. The song was dirty—or maybe dirty is the wrong word for it. It was *sexy*. It was about sex. . . . It was about pleasure in her body and pleasure in someone else's body, and it was coupled with this huge video where she danced and rolled her hips and stroked the taut muscles of some unnamed male dancer.

Janet Jackson appears in concert in 2008. The author refers to Jackson's song "If" as revolutionary in its descriptions of women's sexuality and assertiveness.

It was a song about female desire and sexuality and pleasure that even Madonna hadn't written or performed quite like that. Madonna's sexuality seemed always to be full of hard edges and the tease; Janet's was the pleasure principle in action. She was beautiful and she knew it and she wanted to share all that with a boy that she found beautiful but she wasn't going to sit around hurting herself over him if he wasn't going to come along. She was going to show him exactly what he was missing.

Maybe there's an implied other woman in the song, maybe that's why he can't be with her, but Janet never makes it about another girl. It's between him and her, and it's mostly about her. Take her or leave her, it ain't going to stop her pleasure.

Oh, Janet. That whole album—*janet* [1993]—was like that. If on *Rhythm Nation* she declared that "Someday Is Tonight," on *janet* she'd clearly spent some time having some reallllllly good sex in a way that let her talk about it. The jouissance [pleasure or enjoyment, with a sexual connotation] (forgive me my academic word) was there, was palpable, kept me waiting for the video to come on again.

And when the song turned up eventually on Last.fm this year, it brought back all those feelings. I've turned to it so many times since then, blasted it out of my computer speakers and danced by myself, remembering the freedom it still brought me back then.

(I hear hints of that same feeling in [R&B singer] Beyonce's latest, in "Countdown" especially, that joy-in-being-alive, that pleasure in her own body. It's why I love it.)

Woman-Positive Pop

By the time I learned anything about politics I was well on to punk rock, but I think like language, the messages culture sends you seep in best when you're young, and I think Janet and the rest of these women taught me more about how to handle a world full of land mines for a girl than any book or lecture.

So now, today, when I relish Robyn [a Swedish pop and R&B artist] and Beyoncé and Nicki Minaj, I remember the music that I had as a kid, the pop that didn't need to be underground or indie to be badass, woman-positive, and yes, feminist.

> **EVALUATING THE AUTHOR'S ARGUMENTS:**
>
> Sarah Jaffe suggests at the end of her essay that many contemporary pop and R&B performers are woman-positive and feminist. Does Brandon Soderberg, author of the previous viewpoint, present any evidence to the contrary? Do you think Jaffe and Soderberg would agree about the kind of music that is woman-positive and feminist? Explain your reasoning.

Chapter 3

What Is the Political Effect of Rap Music?

LL Cool J speaks before thousands of New York City public school students at a rally protesting school budget cuts. Rappers are starting to use their influence in politics.

Viewpoint

1

Rap Music Is a Worldwide Form of Political Resistance

Andalusia Knoll, with Scott Pinkelman

"[Hip-hop] allows us to share, it is a means of expression, rebellion and transformation."

Andalusia Knoll is a producer with the national Criminal Justice Dialogue Project Thousand Kites and a reporter for *Free Speech Radio News* and other outlets. In the following viewpoint, she reports on Planeta Rock, a hip-hop festival in Chile. Knoll says that Chilean hip-hop is consciously political and is about building community and encouraging anticapitalist political activism. She concludes by noting that although hip-hop in the United States has become commercial and apolitical, she hopes that hip-hop in Chile will continue to be politically engaged.

AS YOU READ, CONSIDER THE FOLLOWING QUESTIONS:
1. What does Knoll say are the five elements of hip-hop?
2. When did hip-hop arrive in Chile, according to the author?
3. As reported in the viewpoint, why was it difficult to buy a hip-hop CD at the Planeta Rock concert?

In 1982 [early hip-hop artist] Afrika Bambaata dropped the track Planet Rock, a song that brought the words of the Bronx-based *Zulu Nation* [a hip-hop awareness group] to all audiences and was, as hip-hop historian Jeff Chang describes it, a "hypnotic vision of one world under one groove, beyond race, poverty, sociology, and geography." Twenty-eight years later, in 2010, Bambaata's message was alive and well in Santiago, Chile in the form of a week long Hip-Hop Festival aptly named Planeta Rock. Planeta Rock celebrated all the five elements of hip-hop; knowledge, break dancing, graffiti, mc'ing, [or rapping] and djaying. While knowledge is often the forgotten element, it was clear that at Planeta Rock it was the central pillar, where commercialization has yet to influence its form and content, and the lyrics bombast the powers that be.

From Message to Action

The festival opened with the Fiesta Zulu and a message from Afrika Bambaata, sending shout outs from the Bronx down to Santiago and all those that are following in the footsteps of the Zulu Nation. Breakdancers abounded, rocking Six Step, Zulu Spins, and Windmills. This setting could have been anywhere; the break beat pulsed throughout the crowd and hundreds of youth continued to rock it till the wee hours of the night. The political nature and uniqueness of Chilean's political hip-hop scene became more apparent during a release of a book entitled *From Message to Action* that chronicles political hip-hop in Chile. Films shown at the gathering included a smattering of graffiti, music, and break dancing videos from Latin America that were juxtaposed among short political documentaries highlighting land occupations throughout Chile, the plight of political prisoners and the struggles of the indigenous Mapuche people.

At a similar film event at Planeta Rock, a highlight of the night was the music video *1500 dias*, [*1500 Days*] which held a match

FAST FACT

Victor Jara was a Chilean folksinger and a supporter of socialist president Salvador Allende. After the 1973 coup by General Augusto Pinochet, Jara was arrested, tortured, and electrocuted, and his hands and wrists were broken. He was then machine-gunned to death. He was thirty-eight years old.

to all the false campaign promises of the presidential candidates. Just the week before this gathering, the right-wing candidate and media mogul Sebastian Piñera had won the elections. The song lays into the neoliberal policies that all the presidential candidates have pushed, proclaiming that they won't participate in the elections of the rich, and that the 1500 days between elections should serve as 1500 days of organizing and struggle. In a country where 40% of the population is not even registered to vote, these lyrics have widespread resonance.

In Chile, as in many parts of the world, hip-hop is its own form of independent media—the people's resistance to the right-wing controlled media. Regarding this, Dj Erko, one of the organizers of Planeta Rock 2011 referenced a quote by old school NY political group Public Enemy: "As Chuck D said, rap is the CNN of black folks. In our cases it's the CNN of the neighborhood, the barrio of

Rapper Daddy Yankee performs at a hip-hop festival in Chile. Rap music has evolved into a form of political protest and resistance in the country.

the oppressed. Hip-hop has had the capacity to be a tool of contra-information, propaganda, education and knowledge."

In 2011 rappers Subverso and Portavoz, who wrote *1500 days*, have taken their political critique to the next level with the project, *Memoria Rebelde*, or Rebel Memory, which seeks to teach Chilean history through hip-hop and multimedia. Portavoz says the inspiration for this project goes back to the origins of hip-hop. "In the Bronx, Harlem or whichever ghetto, there were many Latin American immigrants and black people who used hip-hop to denounce what was happening and also as a way to share their experiences as black people, as immigrants, and as oppressed people. We are trying to rescue this form of popular education and use rap as a powerful tool to tell the story of our people." They released a *Memoria Rebelde* video at Planeta Rock declaring their refusal to celebrate Chile's bicentennial while thousands of people continue to be oppressed. They also pointed out the government's hypocrisy of celebrating the rescue of 33 miners who had been trapped [in 2010] when the country's history is stained with massacres of miners organizing for workers rights. Subverso says they wrote the song so that people can "recognize the true history of our land and its people" and thank all the "true historians of the people who have been illuminating the dark corners where the poor have struggled to forge their own project of liberation."

Hip-Hop in Chile

If we can learn about the history of Chile through hip-hop, what can we learn about the history of hip-hop in Chile? In many countries where hip-hop is true to its elements, it is a recently-arrived art form. Yet in Chile, hip-hop arrived 25 years ago when the country was living under the brutal dictatorship of President Augusto Pinochet. Pinochet's government came to power in a US backed *coup d'etat* [violent and sudden overthrow of the government] in 1973, which overthrew and assassinated socialist president Salvador Allende and was responsible for the deaths and disappearances of thousands of students, union members, *campesinos* [farmers], intellectuals, leftist politicians, and musicians.

It was in this setting that the first beats of hip-hop trickled down to Chile. Legend has it that one Public Enemy tape arrived and instantly hundreds of copies were made, spreading like wildfire through the *poblaciones* or *poblas* (marginalized neighborhoods) of Santiago, where the lyrics and beats resonated just as they had across the ghettos of the United States. Hip-hop tapes started replacing other tapes by those who secretly listened to Victor Jara, Inti Illimani, and other folk music of the *Nueva Canción* [New Song] movement that had been on heavy rotation among the dictatorship's resistance. Hip-hop ceased being a clandestine art form, when classic hip-hop films *Beat Street* and *Breakdance* aired on national television and break dancing entered the public consciousness. Shortly thereafter, breakers hit the street corners in downtown Santiago, contorting their bodies and dancing moves the people had never seen before, but instantly wanted to emulate. Following the spread of break dancing, certain Chilean hip-hop groups broke out on the scene including *Panteras Negras* [Black Panthers], who clearly took inspiration from the US-based Black Liberation movement and a few years later Makiza, that featured the currently globally popular Anita Tijoux who performs at Planeta Rock every year.

Hip-Hop Anticapitalism

Bufonk is an MC[1] who has been involved with various hip-hop collectives over the years. He and his brother, who is also the well known MC Guerrillero Okulto, grew up in a "*tomada*," an urban land occupation, where many of Santiago's poorest people lived, in shacks, without running water, electricity and general city infrastructure. Pinochet not only repressed all leftist dissent but also ushered in neoliberal reforms, which privatized businesses expropriated by the Allende government, lowered wages and encouraged foreign bank loans. The beneficiaries of this new economy—including Pinochet and his family—became known as the piranhas and made millions while the majority of Chileans saw their standard of living drop. These policies were continued after the military government, and today Chile's export-oriented economy is one of the most unequal in Latin America.

When I asked Bufonk why the hip-hop scene and lyrics were so anticapitalist he responded. "The poverty that we experienced was a

---

1. Derived from the original abbreviation for "master of ceremonies" (MC); now used as a generic term for a performer who speaks over a beat or performs songs in the hip-hop and rap music genres.

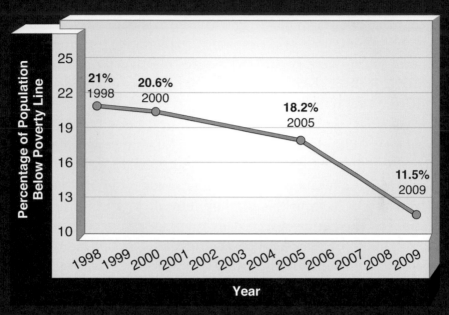

Taken from: Index Mundi, "Population Below Poverty Line (Chile)," Historical Data Graphs per Year, January 11, 2011. www.indexmundi.com/g/g.aspx?c=ci&v=69. Data source: CIA World Factbook.

direct result of neoliberalism and capitalism. Living in those conditions, how could we then turn around and perpetuate capitalism?"

Not only do many Chilean hip-hop artists rap about the injustices inherent in the new world order, but they also manifest it in the way they organize concerts, events and share music. At Planeta Rock, it was easier to buy an ice cream than a hip-hop CD, as most share their music through free downloads on the Internet.

Lah Tere, a member of the US based Afro-Boricuan/Chilean hip-hop trio Rebel Diaz performed at Planeta Rock in 2010. She said "This doesn't even happen in the Bronx where hip-hop started. The youth aren't connected like they are here with hip-hop and knowledge. Everywhere you look there is a cypher [group] going on with kids b-boxing [beatboxing, using the voice to create the sound of percussion instruments] and rapping. There is true leadership, loyalty, pride and people are excited about their culture and participate in things." . . .

Will Hip-Hop Be Co-Opted?

When one views this huge do-it-yourself political hip-hop movement, it's hard to not wonder if it will meet the same sad fate as hip-hop in the US, where messages of struggle have been silenced and taken over by the bling-bling of a hyper capitalist, exploitative hip-hop market. Habitual [an mc and organizer] assures me that won't happen to them: "Capitalism always tries to co-opt subcultures and drive it in a certain direction to function in its interest. The market is always looking to where it can drink more blood—but we don't agree with the market logic." He adds, "Hip Hop reflects values that we identify with to transform the logic of capitalism and social relationships. It allows us to share, it is a means of expression, rebellion and transformation."

If you step back from this hip-hop movement and think of Chile at large, and the battles waged daily by Mapuche people on hunger strikes fighting for their land and culture, students filling the streets against rising tuition, and then walk the streets of Santiago passing by the radical political sloganeering graffiti that dots every street corner, you can imagine that as long as the people keep fighting, political anticapitalist hip-hop will thrive and grow.

EVALUATING THE AUTHOR'S ARGUMENTS:

Do you think Andalusia Knoll would agree with Liz Funk's distinction between hip-hop and rap presented in chapter 2, viewpoint 3? Would Funk (or Knoll) characterize Planeta Rock as an example of hip-hop or rap? Would Sarah Jaffe, author of the previous viewpoint, agree with Knoll that the political impact of rappers (such as Nicki Minaj) has largely been undermined in the United States? Explain your answers.

Rap Music Is Not Politically Thoughtful or Effective

John H. McWhorter

"I think that the idea that hip-hop is devoted to political change is mistaken. . . . Hip-hop is devoted to dissing authority for its own sake."

John H. McWhorter is a linguist, political commentator, senior fellow at the Manhattan Institute, and lecturer at Columbia University. In the following viewpoint, he argues that rap music does not make thoughtful political points. Instead, he says, hip-hop simply attacks authority. As an example, he points to rapper KRS-One, who in one song says that there are not enough jobs for black people. McWhorter contends that this ignores numerous programs and initiatives that have increased black employment. He characterizes KRS-One's politics as simplistic and counterproductive.

AS YOU READ, CONSIDER THE FOLLOWING QUESTIONS:

1. What does McWhorter say he likes about the Marley Marl album *Hip Hop Lives*?
2. What does the author say is the implication of the line "Employment is stallin' us"?
3. What is the first "job creation program" McWhorter discusses?

The party line is that hip-hop is telling it like it is, showing us where to go, hitting the sweet spot as it hasn't been hit since somewhere between Martin Luther King and [black power advocate and leader of the Black Panther Party] Huey Newton. Ethnomusicologist Cheryl Keyes tells us that "rap music serves as a political forum," and that "artists utilize rap as a discursive tool through which to discuss social and political issues." Michael Eric Dyson, black Georgetown professor and today's most prominent academic supporter of hip-hop, writes that "when rappers argue over scarce resources for their poor brothers and sisters, and question why poor black folk don't share in the economic and social bounty of mainstream America, they are also behaving politically." Sports journalist Dave Zirin thinks hip-hop "has the capacity to threaten power like no other art form. When Kanye West said on national TV [in 2005] that George [W.] Bush doesn't care about black people, it created an unholy stir. If his stage mate at the time, the slack-jawed Mike Myers, or even another prominent African American, like Denzel Washington, had said the same, the reception would have been profoundly different."

Hip-Hop Is About Attitude, Not Politics

Keyes, Zirin, and Dyson see their statements as logic pure and simple. Yet I have a hard time seeing a clear relationship between the way they describe rap and the music one actually hears—"conscious" or not.

The question is not whether rappers mention famous figures and current events. The question is what the overall intent is. I think that the idea that hip-hop is devoted to political change is mistaken, even when "serious." Hip-hop is devoted to dissing authority for its own sake.

Why can't it be both, you might ask: why can't music that is all about attitude also be politically useful? The reason is that the game is at heart the attitude, making it too easy to miss what creates actual change. Activism and acting up are not the same thing.

To show you what I mean, I will start with KRS-One and Marley Marl's latest album *Hip Hop Lives*. It's a good example of how "hip-hop politics" is not *constructive* politics, because the album is really all about the upturned middle finger for the sake of atmosphere.

As good music, there is so much to love about *Hip Hop Lives* that it's hard to know where to start. I like KRS's line about having been present at the birth of all of his children in "I Was There." On that cut, I like the way he delivers the refrain "Where were *you*?" with an intonation impossible to get down on paper but that articulately captures a tone of challenge; it's less a question than a jab. It's percussion. Verbal percussion is fun to listen to. "Musika" suggests a black-Latino alliance, and nicely rhymes *ghetto* not with standard Spanish *esto* ("this") but with the common colloquial pronunciation "eh'to." I like it when DJ Premier "walks in" and the rhythm track for "The Victory" is one of his typical spare, jazzy little grooves.

But if you listen to the album with your head rather than your heart, it's hard to see KRS-One as leading us anywhere useful.

KRS-One seems to think he has it all figured out: "We keep showin' you, and showin' you, and showin' you." But the politics are static.

KRS-One and Jobs

"Employment is stallin' us," he tells us. The implication is that there aren't enough jobs for black people, or more specifically black people from the 'hood. That is, jobs need to be created for poor blacks.

Unemployment for Blacks and Whites Since the Start of the Great Recession

Unemployment rate for . . .	Fourth Quarter 2007 (percent)	Second Quarter 2009 (percent)	Second Quarter 2011 (percent)	Difference between African Americans and whites for respective groups in second quarter 2011 (in percentage points)
African Americans	8.4	14.8	16.1	8.2
Whites	4.0	8.3	7.9	

Note: All unemployment rates are in percent. In the column at far right, the change in the difference between African Americans and whites is expressed in percentage points.

Taken from: Christian E. Weller and Jaryn Fields, "The Black and White Labor Gap in America," Center for American Progress, July 25, 2011. www.americanprogress.org. Calculations based on Bureau of Labor Statistics, Current Population Survey, (US Department of Labor, 2011).

However, at what point in black history has job creation actually borne any lasting fruit? Can anyone come up with two or three examples of where that was done and if it created major change in black communities? Not summer jobs for teenagers, although the record on that is hardly stellar either, but real jobs, for grown-ups, to work year-round?

Let's turn down *Hip Hop Lives* for a second. Down, down—hear those beats fading away. We'll turn it back up in a bit, but here is a time-out on employment, black people, and low education.

I know of three jobs-creation systems that are changing black communities. None of them are on KRS-One's mind.

Jobs Creation Program One

In 1996, welfare was changed from an open-ended entitlement that basically paid women to have children, into a job training program with a five-year time limit. Since then, the welfare rolls have dropped by 60 percent, and single mothers have been getting jobs in numbers unknown since the seventies. Not as corporate executives, but they are working. The number of black children living in poverty took a sharp dip in 1996. The old chestnut that 41 percent of black children live in poverty is obsolete: the number today is 30 percent. Welfare reform was, in its way, a revolution for black people.

Jobs Creation Program Two

Around the country, organizations are giving urban black and brown people without college degrees aged eighteen to twenty-four the tools to find and keep steady work. For example, after five years of operation in 2005, 90 percent of the at-risk people who had gone through the program Year Up in Boston were still working. The program now has branches in Washington, D.C., Providence, and New York. America Works places former welfare recipients into jobs. Half of the clients have no high school diplomas; most score academically at an eighth-grade level. After placing clients in jobs for a training period, America Works remains their formal employer, helping the client acclimate to the work environment. Three years after placement, 88 percent of America Works clients are still off welfare. America Works has branches in Manhattan, Brooklyn, Queens, Albany, Baltimore, and Oakland. America Works was also, for the record, founded by white people.

Jobs Creation Program Three

The Bush administration (yes, them) has for years been channeling funds to churches under the Faith-Based and Community Initiatives program. One pilot program supervised by the Department of Labor called Ready4Work was successful at bringing ex-cons back into society and getting them jobs, with religious faith an integral part of keeping people on the straight path. Because of this success, a bill taking prisoner re-entry national is working its way through Congress, called the Second Chance Act. In cities, most returning prisoners are black men on their way back to the inner-city communities they came from.

A Misstatement of the Problem

To be interested in black unemployment is to attend to things such as the above.

And now, let's turn the volume back up on KRS-One: "Employment is stallin' us." This will not do. Is KRS-One aware that employment rates among poor black women are climbing? Is KRS-One interested in philanthropic, grassroots and government-funded organizations getting black men off the streets and into office jobs?

One might object that I am putting too much responsibility on what is, in the end, just one line in one rap on one album. But it is exactly this kind of line that has people thinking of hip-hop as politically significant, and it is misleading. When KRS-One raps

The author says that rapper KRS-One (pictured) and others ignore numerous programs and initiatives that have increased black employment and argues that KRS-One's politics are counterproductive.

"Employment is stallin' us," he plants a bug in rap fans' ears that black activism should be about decrying that there is no work available for poor black people—such that in the film *Dave Chappelle's Block Party*, a sweet young black girl, asked how she would change the country, says that she would have there be more jobs and gets applauded. But that is a misstatement of the problem.

EVALUATING THE AUTHOR'S ARGUMENTS:

Would John H. McWhorter agree with Andalusia Knoll, author of the previous viewpoint, that the activism at Planeta Rock in Chile is constructive or worthwhile? Would he agree with Sarah Jaffe's position in chapter 2, viewpoint 6, that songs by Janet Jackson or Salt-n-Pepa are politically positive? What sort of art or music, if any, do you think McWhorter would consider to be politically relevant? Explain your answers.

Rap's Promotion of Capitalism and Success Is Dangerous

"The real problem with rap is that far from undermining society's values it's reinforcing them."

Dreda Say Mitchell

Dreda Say Mitchell is a British crime novelist. In the following viewpoint, she argues that most rap music does not focus on violence, but on wealth. She says that this focus on wealth encourages young people to believe that their self-worth is tied to the amount of money they have. She argues that this obsession with money is especially destructive for the working class. It is the obsession with money throughout culture, not a focus on violence in rap, that causes the frustration and violence in society, says Mitchell.

AS YOU READ, CONSIDER THE FOLLOWING QUESTIONS:
1. According to Mitchell, what "usual suspects" are accused of causing youth to "go off the rails"?
2. What does the author say is the standard image that emerges from watching rap videos?
3. Why does Mitchell believe that the money and success ethic of rap will not harm middle-class youth?

If the nation's youth are going off the rails—and a flip through the newspaper archives suggests they have been since the 1950s—then clearly something must be to blame. The usual suspects are, in no particular order, capitalism, liberalism, consumerism, and family breakdown. But particularly after the shooting of young men at the Notting Hill Carnival on Monday evening, the debate inevitably turns to music.

Ask any youth in our cities, irrespective of ethnic background, about rap and you'll get a roll of the eyes—they're more than familiar with this argument—and you'll be told you're taking it too seriously, it's just showbiz. No one's embracing a gun and gang culture because of anything they've seen on television or heard on their MP3, there are other forces at work. Nor, sadly, do they think there's much anyone can do about it, it's just "how it is".

Music, along with many other factors, helps to set the tone for what is considered acceptable behaviour in our society. But there's no doubt that our "culture" in its broadest sense legitimises, or otherwise,

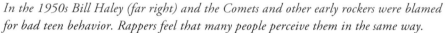

In the 1950s Bill Haley (far right) and the Comets and other early rockers were blamed for bad teen behavior. Rappers feel that many people perceive them in the same way.

certain actions or attitudes. Music does form an important part of youth culture, so it's a fair question to ask whether music has an influence. But it's always been easier to assume there's a link than actually demonstrate one. Few people now would want to blame poor old Bill Haley in "Rock Around the Clock" for teenagers trashing cinemas in the 1950s, but people certainly did at the time.

Rockers have had their day as a threat to the nation's young. If you're bang up to date, you're blaming rap, specifically gangsta rap, for guns and gangs. And at first sight you might seem to have a point. When news crews shoot footage of the latest tragedy on our streets, the youths involved look like characters from rap videos, they use the same slang and they seem to echo the same attitudes. So is it case closed?

But rap is not homogenous—there are individual rappers and the music they make. Some of the music is so relentlessly "positive" that it would get the thumbs up from any worry coven. At the other end of the spectrum, there's no denying that a minority of rappers, often under commercial pressure to be "badder" than the rest and believing their own hype and publicity, do end up in murky waters.

In fact there's very little violence or guns in mainstream rap. Spend an evening watching rap videos (and it's difficult to believe that many people who worry about it actually have) and a fairly standard image starts to emerge. There'll be the stars by a swimming pool, in a fast car or a flashy club, wearing designer clothes and jewellery, surrounded by a half a dozen, purely decorative, "honeyz." The message (in as far as there is one) that you'll pick up from this is simple—that if you're not loaded, you're not happening. And it's not hard to see why record companies and other corporations don't have a problem with that, because that's exactly what they believe too.

The real problem with rap is that far from undermining society's values it's reinforcing them, and the most fundamental of all our society's values at the moment is that you are what you own. Commercial rap's money and success ethic won't do any harm to middle-class youth; they have access to the professions and property where they can participate in it. For working-class youngsters, taught by our culture since the 1970s that they're losers and failures, it's part of a profoundly poisonous cocktail of attitudes. Pride and self-respect are at the heart of this debate and it's the lack of those, or the wrong sort, that's really driving the violence on our streets.

Respectable society expects those involved in street culture to start taking responsibility for what they do, and change their behaviour and attitudes. No argument there, but it's equally true that the rest of us

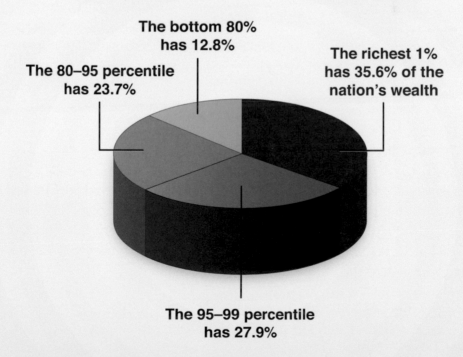

Distribution of US Wealth, 2009

The bottom 80% has 12.8%

The richest 1% has 35.6% of the nation's wealth

The 80–95 percentile has 23.7%

The 95–99 percentile has 27.9%

Taken from: Inequality.org, "Wealth Inequality," based on Economic Policy Institute data, 2011.
http://inequality.org/wealth-inequality.

might want to think about taking responsibility for what we do, and changing the behaviour and attitudes that creates the environment our youth live in. In Britain in 2007 though, that's an unfashionable attitude. Most of us think we're stuck with the society we've got because "that's how it is . . ."

EVALUATING THE AUTHOR'S ARGUMENTS:

Would Andalusia Knoll, author of the first viewpoint in chapter 3, agree with Dreda Say Mitchell that the ethic of success in mainstream Western rap is harmful? Would the author of the previous viewpoint, John H. McWhorter, agree? What arguments might these authors use to defend their positions?

Viewpoint

4

Rap's Promotion of Capitalism and Success Is Healthy

Steve Yates

"The story of hip-hop's journey into the cultural mainstream is the story of its love affair with materialism, or, more accurately, capitalism."

Steve Yates is a British music journalist, writer, and editor. In the following viewpoint, he says that many critics attack rap music for its materialism. He argues, however, that hip-hop's focus on materialism and capitalism is what allowed it to become mainstream music at the center of American culture. He says that a focus on success does have some downsides. However, Yates concludes that encouraging people to improve their lives is ultimately positive and helpful.

AS YOU READ, CONSIDER THE FOLLOWING QUESTIONS:

1. As reported by Yates, how does Darren Wright explain hip-hop's appeal to corporate brands?
2. With what business did Percy "Master P" Miller start out, and what did that business grow into, according to the author?
3. How does Yates say that Barack Obama symbolized hip-hop's move to America's core?

For its detractors . . . materialism is one of rap's three deadly sins, along with its violence and misogyny [hatred toward women]. Casual fans of hip-hop often see its materialistic side as something either to be played down or embraced "ironically." Some commentators judge it more harshly. When the riots broke out across Britain this summer [August 2011, in which more than 3,000 people were arrested], many saw hip-hop's celebration of materialism as one of the key causes. Paul Routledge, writing in [the British newspaper] the *Mirror*, summarised this view when he said, "I blame the pernicious culture of hatred around rap music, which glorifies violence and loathing of authority . . . [and] exalts trashy materialism."

Hip-Hop and Capitalism

Routledge is not *entirely* wrong. The story of hip-hop's journey into the cultural mainstream is the story of its love affair with materialism, or, more accurately, capitalism. Its lead exponents, like Jay-Z and Kanye West, are brilliant entrepreneurs with vast fortunes (even if their music advocates a profligacy [extravagance] that is anathema to [disliked by] the savvy business operator). Hip-hop's rise has been, at root, a straightforward process of free-market enterprise: an excellent product has been pushed with great skill and new markets opened up with real dynamism and flair.

Unsurprisingly, corporate brands have been keen to get involved. Darren Wright, creative director of the Nike account at advertising agency Wieden+Kennedy explains the appeal: "With hip hop you're buying more than music. It isn't a genre—it's a lifestyle, encompassing fashion, break dancing, the clothes or the jewels you wear. . . . The lifestyle is worth its weight in gold because it's not just about one rap song, it's so much more."

The view of hip-hop as a genre concerned only with the basest forms of materialism is a serious oversimplification. It misunderstands the way that rap's relationship with capitalism has fed its creativity and led to both its commercial and artistic success.

Conscious, Gangsta, Mainstream

While modern hip-hop is unashamedly materialistic, its ancestors were different. As far back as the 1960s, artists such as *The Last Poets* and Gil Scott-Heron combined African American music with spoken word

Rap's Top Earners, August 2010 to July 2011

Performer	Earnings
Jay-Z	$37 million
Diddy	$35 million
Lil Wayne	$15 million
Dr. Dre	$14 million
Eminem	$14 million
Snoop Dogg	$14 million

Taken from: Zack O'Malley, "Cash Kings 2011: Hip-Hop's Top Earners." *Forbes*, August 9, 2011.

poetry. But Scott-Heron, like others of that generation, was critical of the passive materialism that he saw working its way into black culture. As he intoned on "The Revolution Will Not Be Televised": "The revolution will not go better with Coke / The revolution will not fight the germs that may cause bad breath / The revolution will put you in the driver's seat." This political consciousness was taken up in the 1980s by the extraordinary Public Enemy, a New York group that mixed incendiary politics with apocalyptic music, militaristic dress and cartoon humour. Gentler, but still political, takes on "Afrocentricity" were advanced by the brilliant Native Tongues collective including groups like De La Soul, A Tribe Called Quest and the Jungle Brothers.

But by the early 1990s, this "conscious" streak was being eclipsed by the giddy thrills of gangsta rap. Its motivation was pithily [concisely] summarised by NWA (Niggaz With Attitude), the group who named and codified the subgenre, on their track "Gangsta Gangsta"—"life ain't nothin' but bitches and money." Despite this apparent nihilism, NWA embraced the American dream with relish. They set down the unapologetic "money-is-all" credo of the low-level street hustler, in which drug dealing, guns and the police swirl about in a ferocious urban storm. Like other popular representations of American gangsterism—*The Godfather*, *Scarface*—it was a vision of unfettered free market enterprise.

Slowly, the early political message was replaced by this focus on accumulation, both in the lyrics and also the business practices of those who were running the scene. One of hip-hop's key entrepreneurs was Percy "Master P" Miller, who grew his No Limit empire from an LA record shop into a record label and then into a conglomerate. Miller spearheaded a new wave of hip-hop business by entering into joint ventures with music companies. He chose Priority, which was independent of the major record labels, and which had made a packet out of NWA and other leading artists. His deal brought all the benefits of working for major labels, such as distribution and marketing muscle, without the drawbacks— Master P was able to retain copyright control over the music and release records to his own schedule.

But not content with music, he diversified wildly: clothing, property, Master P dolls—even telephone sex lines. His debut film, the low-budget, straight-to-video *I'm Bout It* (1997) raked in sales that would have satisfied major studios. In 1998, Miller's companies grossed $160m[illion].

In New York, the business interests of Sean "Puff Daddy" Combs developed along parallel lines: music, restaurants, a magazine, the inevitable clothing line, all name-stamped in a manner that led the consumer back to the man himself. Dan Charnas, in his masterful book *The Big Payback: The History Of The Business Of Hip-Hop*, describes Miller and Combs as "the embodiment of the superpowered artist, two one-man brands, the fulfilment of [the] vision of self-determination and ownership—not just for hip-hop artists, not just for black artists, but for all American artists." Having turned their art into business, they turned their business back into art. According to Charnas, their success "would mark the beginning of an unprecedented spike in black American entrepreneurship."

Rapper-turned-mogul Sean "Puff Daddy" Combs stands with models at the launch of his women's clothing line. Embracing the "money is all" credo of rap, which began in the early 1990s, Combs has developed business interests that include music, restaurants, a magazine, and men's and women's fashions.

An Intimate Relationship with Business

So while hip-hop started off as an underground, and often political movement, it has for many years pursued an increasingly intimate relationship with business. Hip-hop now has a materialist, acquisitive streak hard-wired into its identity. It is this embrace of capitalism that has taken hip-hop from outsider status right to America's core. This ascent was neatly symbolised when Barack Obama, on the [presidential] nomination campaign trail in 2008, dismissed criticisms from the [rival candidate Hillary] Clinton camp by mimicking Jay-Z's famous "dirt off my shoulder" gesture. Asked which rappers were on his iPod, there was only one candidate. . . .

Success and Independence

In the past 30-or-so years, hip-hop has tried politics and it has tried gangsterism. But in the end it settled for capitalism, which energised it and brought it to a position of global dominance. American rappers like Puff Daddy and Master P, men who fought their way into the big time, did so by selling a vision of independence, empowerment and material success. That vision is also found, if less vividly, in Britain's rap music. And though hip-hop retains unpleasant features, the core message, that people can have better lives, is incontestably a good one.

EVALUATING THE AUTHOR'S ARGUMENTS:

Steve Yates says at the end of his viewpoint that the core message of materialistic hip-hop is that people "can have better lives." How does hip-hop define "better lives," according to Yates? Would the authors of chapter three viewpoints 1 and 3, Andalusia Knoll and Dreda Say Mitchell, respectively, agree with this definition of "better lives"? Do you agree with it? Why or why not?

Facts About Rap Music

Editor's note: These facts can be used in reports or papers to reinforce or add credibility when making important points or claims.

Early History of Rap Music

According to Henry A. Rhodes, writing at the Yale-New Haven Teachers Institute:

- One of the major influences on rap music was Jamaican toasting. In toasting, a DJ would shout slogans or rhymes over an R&B record.
- Jamaican DJs also used a technique called dubbing, in which DJs would cut back and forth between vocal and instrumental tracks and adjust the bass and treble.
- The Jamaican traditions of toasting and dubbing were brought to the Bronx in New York by Clive Campbell, known as Kool Herc, in the early 1970s. This was the beginning of rap music and hip-hop.
- A DJ known as Theodor invented the technique of "scratching," in which a DJ spins a record back and forth underneath the needle, creating a percussive, rhythmic sound.

According to Henry Adaso, a music journalist writing at About.com:

- The first rap hit was "Rapper's Delight" by the Sugarhill Gang, which went to number thirty-six on the *Billboard* charts in 1979.
- The first record to capture the sound of a live DJ scratching was "The Adventures of Grandmaster Flash," released in 1980.
- Rapper Ice-T released the singles "Body Rock" and "Killers" in 1983, helping to pioneer gangsta rap.
- Public Enemy released their album *Yo! Bum Rush the Show* in 1987. It was a landmark in politically conscious hip-hop.
- Rap received its own show on MTV in 1988, signaling greater mainstream interest in the music.

- In 1991 hip-hop group N.W.A's gangsta rap album *Niggaz4life* sold more than 954,000 copies in its first week of release and reached number one on the pop charts. Gangsta rap would henceforth be massively popular.

Significant Rap Albums

According to *Rolling Stone* magazine's list of the five hundred greatest albums of all time, published in 2003, the twenty-five greatest rap albums are:

25. Public Enemy, *Yo! Bum Rush the Show* (1987)
24. The Notorious B.I.G., *Life After Death* (1997)
23. L.L. Cool J, *Radio* (1985)
22. Fugees, *The Score* (1996)
21. Jay-Z, *The Blueprint* (2001)
20. Nas, *Illmatic* (1994)
19. Wu-Tang Clan, *Enter the Wu-Tang (36 Chambers)* (1993)
18. Outkast, *Stankonia* (2000)
17. De La Soul, *3 Feet High and Rising* (1989)
16. Eminem, *The Eminem Show* (2002)
15. Lauryn Hill, *The Miseducation of Lauryn Hill* (1998)
14. Eminem, *The Marshall Mathers LP* (2000)
13. Public Enemy, *Fear of a Black Planet* (1990)
12. Eminem, *The Slim Shady LP* (1999)
11. Jay-Z, *Reasonable Doubt* (1996)
10. Run-D.M.C., *Run-D.M.C.* (1984)
9. Eric B. and Rakim, *Paid in Full* (1987)
8. Beastie Boys, *Licensed to Ill* (1986)
7. Beastie Boys, *Paul's Boutique* (1989)
6. A Tribe Called Quest, *The Low End Theory* (1991)
5. N.W.A., *Straight Outta Compton* (1988)
4. Dr. Dre, *The Chronic* (1992)
3. The Notorious B.I.G., *Ready to Die* (1994)
2. Run-D.M.C., *Raising Hell* (1986)
1. Public Enemy, *It Takes a Nation of Millions to Hold Us Back* (1988)

According to the Recording Industry Association of America, the following are the ten best-selling hip-hop albums of all time:

1. Outkast, *Speakerboxxx/The Love Below* (2003): 11 million sold
2. Eminem, *The Marshall Mathers LP* (2000): 10.4 million sold
3. Eminem, *The Eminem Show* (2002): 10 million sold.
4. The Notorious B.I.G., *Life After Death* (1997): 10 million sold.
5. MC Hammer, *Please Hammer Don't Hurt 'Em* (1990): 10 million sold
6. Tupac Shakur, *Greatest Hits* (1998): 10 million sold
7. Tupac Shakur, *All Eyez on Me* (1996): 9 million sold
8. Beastie Boys, *Licensed to Ill* (1986): 9 million sold
9. Will Smith, *Big Willie Style* (1997): 9 million sold
10. 50 Cent, *Get Rich or Die Tryin'* (2003): 9 million sold

American Opinions on Rap and Hip-Hop Music
According to a 2007 poll by the Pew Research Center:

- Five percent of all adults said rap is having a good influence on society.
- Seventy-one percent said it is having a bad influence.
- Sixteen percent said it is not having much influence.
- Eight percent were unsure.

- Four percent of white adults said rap is having a good influence on society.
- Seventy-four percent said it is having a bad influence.
- Fourteen percent said it is not having much influence.
- Eight percent were unsure.

- Six percent of black adults said rap is having a good influence on society.
- Seventy-one percent said it is having a bad influence.
- Sixteen percent said it is not having much influence.
- Seven percent were unsure.

- Fourteen percent of Hispanic adults said rap is having a good influence on society.
- Forty-eight percent said it is having a bad influence.
- Twenty-one percent said it is not having much influence.
- Seventeen percent were unsure.

- Eight percent of all adults said hip-hop is having a good influence on society.
- Sixty-two percent said it is having a bad influence.
- Seventeen percent said it is not having much influence.
- Thirteen percent were unsure.

- Six percent of white adults said hip-hop is having a good influence on society.
- Sixty-four percent said it is having a bad influence.
- Seventeen percent said it is not having much influence.
- Thirteen percent were unsure.

- Thirteen percent of black adults said hip-hop is having a good influence on society.
- Sixty-one percent said it is having a bad influence.
- Eighteen percent said it is not having much influence.
- Eight percent were unsure.

- Ten percent of Hispanic adults said hip-hop is having a good influence on society.
- Fifty-nine percent said it is having a bad influence.
- Twenty-three percent said it is not having much influence.
- Eight percent were unsure.

Organizations to Contact

The editors have compiled the following list of organizations concerned with the issues debated in this book. The descriptions are derived from materials provided by the organizations. All have publications or information available for interested readers. The list was compiled on the date of publication of the present volume; the information provided here may change. Be aware that many organizations take several weeks or longer to respond to inquiries, so allow as much time as possible for the receipt of requested materials.

Center for Media Literacy (CML)
23852 Pacific Coast Hwy., #472
Malibu, CA 90265
(310) 456-1225
fax: (310) 456-0020
e-mail: cml@medialit.org
website: www.medialit.org

The CML seeks to increase critical analysis of the media through its publication of educational materials, including MediaLit Kits, which provide a framework for introducing media literacy in schools and community groups. The center was founded on the belief that media literacy is an essential skill in the twenty-first century as varying media forms become increasingly common in everyday life and that individuals should be empowered from a young age to make informed choices about the media they consume. *Connections* is the official newsletter of the organization, with archival issues available online. Additional informative materials can be browsed by topic on the CML website, which includes several articles on media violence.

Concerned Women for America (CWA)
1015 Fifteenth St. NW, Ste. 1100
Washington, DC 20005
(202) 488-7000

fax: (202) 448-0806
e-mail: mail@cwfa.org
website: www.cwfa.org

The CWA seeks to protect the interests of American families, promote biblical values, and provide a voice for women throughout the United States who believe in Judeo-Christian values. The CWA believes that sexually explicit popular culture contributes to the decline of families and interferes with raising healthy children. The CWA publishes the periodic publication *Family Voice* and numerous press releases and reports, including "Sexually Explicit Media and Children" and "Music's Deadly Influence."

Culture Shock

2110 Hancock St., Ste. 200
San Diego, CA 92110
(619) 299-2110
e-mail: angiebunch@cultureshockdance.org
website: www.cultureshockdance.org

Culture Shock is a network of nonprofit hip-hop dance companies dedicated to offering children and youth in diverse communities an alternative to street life by providing a rewarding activity and instilling confidence. Founded in 1993, Culture Shock has grown from its home location of San Diego, California, to cities across the United States, Canada, and the United Kingdom.

Heritage Foundation

214 Massachusetts Ave. NE
Washington, DC 20002-4999
(202) 546-4400 • toll-free: (800) 544-4843
fax: (202) 546-8328
e-mail: info@heritage.org
website: www.heritage.org

The Heritage Foundation is a conservative public policy organization dedicated to individual liberty, free-market principles, and limited gov- ernment. It advises parents to restrict the music and movies that chil- dren and youth consume. Its resident scholars publish position papers on a wide range of issues, including "A Culture Awash in Porn" and "The Culture War: A Five-Point Plan for Parents."

Hip-Hop Association (H2A)
PO Box 1181
New York, NY 10035
(718) 682-2744
fax: (866) 540-0384
e-mail: info@hiphopassociation.org
website: www.hiphopassociation.org

Founded in 2002, the H2A works to facilitate critical thinking and to foster constructive social change and unity to instill tolerance, civic participation, social reform, and economic sustainability, while advancing hip-hop culture through innovative programming. The H2A organizes an international film festival and publishes the monthly *Defuse News*, a news and information report that includes commentary, announcements, and resources such as grants, fellowships, and job opportunities.

Hip-Hop Theater Festival (HHTF)
442-D Lorimer St., #195
Brooklyn, NY 11206
(718) 497-4282
fax: (718) 497-4240
e-mail: info@hhtf.org
website: www.hhtf.org

The mission of the HHTF is to promote hip-hop theater as a recognized genre by commissioning and developing new works and helping artists build coalitions, collaborations, and networks with other artists and institutions in the United States and around the world. The organization presents live events created by artists who combine a variety of theatrical forms, including theater, dance, spoken word, and live music sampling. The HHTF also strives to bring new, younger audiences to the theater in large numbers, in an effort to ensure the future of live performance.

Hip-Hop Summit Action Network (HSAN)
e-mail: info@hsan.org
wesbsite: www.hsan.org

The HSAN is dedicated to using hip-hop music to serve as a catalyst for education advocacy and youth empowerment. It sponsors hip-hop summits, organizes voter registration drives, and engages in leadership development. Its website includes news releases and information about HSAN programs and activities.

Morality in Media (MIM)
475 Riverside Dr., Ste. 1264
New York, NY 10115
(212) 870-3222
fax: (212) 870-2765
e-mail: mim@moralityinmedia.org
website: www.moralityinmedia.org

The MIM is an interfaith organization that fights pornography and opposes indecency in the mainstream media. It maintains the National Obscenity Law Center, a clearinghouse of legal materials on obscenity law. The MIM publishes the quarterly *Morality in Media Newsletter* and the bimonthly *Obscenity Law Bulletin* and several papers, including "Hip-Hop Misogyny: A Destructive Force," "Altered Perceptions—Media and Youth," and "Mass Murder and Popular Culture."

For Further Reading

Books

Bradley, Adam. *Book of Rhymes: The Poetics of Hip-Hop*. New York: BasicCivitas, 2009. Examines the literary achievement of rap, looking closely at many of the genre's most famous lyrics.

Charnas, Dan. *The Big Payback: The History of the Business of Hip-Hop*. New York: Penguin, 2010. A history of the business aspects of hip-hop, from its beginnings to its massive later success.

Forman, Murray, and Mark Anthony Neal, eds. *That's the Joint! The Hip-Hop Studies Reader*. 2nd ed. New York: Routledge, 2011. A collection of hip-hop scholarship, focusing on social activism, aesthetics, the industry, and many other topics.

Ogbar, Jeffrey O.G. *Hip-Hop Revolution: The Culture and Politics of Rap*. Lawrence: University of Kansas Press, 2007. Discusses the ways in which ideas about hip-hop authenticity affect rap music and presentation.

Rose, Tricia. *The Hip Hop Wars: What We Talk About When We Talk About Hip Hop—and Why It Matters*. New York: BasicCivitas, 2006. Argues that hip-hop has become one of the primary ways in which Americans talk about race. It explores and critiques arguments for and against hip-hop.

Periodicals and Internet Sources

Abrams, Jim. "Hearing Criticizes Sex, Violence in Hip-Hop," *USA Today*, September 25, 2007. www.usatoday.com/life/music/news/2007-09-25-hip-hop-congress_N.htm.

Ali, Aisha. "Hip-Hop Meets Its Ultimate Fate: Hip-Hop Surrenders to Capitalism (Dollar Dollar Bill, Ya'll)," Examiner.com, May 4, 2009. www.examiner.com/dc-in-washington-dc/hip-hop-meets-its-ultimate-fate-hip-hop-surrenders-to-capitalism-dollar-dollar-bill-ya-ll.

Anderson, Amanda. "Sexism in Hip Hop: Why Must Female Emcees Be Philosophical, but Male Emcees Don't?," *Urban Belle*, November 8, 2010. www.urbanbellemag.com/2010/11/sexism-in-hip-hop-why-must-female.html.

Bartow, Ann. "Hip Hop, Capitalism, and Taking Back the Music," *Feminist Law Professors* (blog), December 9, 2008. www.feminist lawprofessors.com/2008/12/4419/.

Chapin, Bernard. "Rap Music Holds Blacks Down," *Strike the Root*, July 24, 2003. www.strike-the-root.com/3/chapin/chapin18.html.

Cook, John. "Blacklisted: Is Stephin Merritt a Racist Because He Doesn't Like Hip-Hop?," *Slate*, May 9, 2006. www.slate.com /articles/arts/music_box/2006/05/blacklisted.html.

Haaretz. "Auschwitz Survivor and Turkish Rapper Team Up to Fight Racism," January 26, 2010. www.haaretz.com/jewish-world /news/auschwitz-survivor-and-turkish-rapper-team-up-to-fight -racism-1.262124.

Jacobson, Mark. "WorldStar, Baby!," *New York*, February 5, 2012. http://nymag.com/news/features/worldstar-2012-2.

Johnson, Jeff. "'Cousin Jeff': Don't Blame Hip-Hop for Society's Sexism," CNN, May 7, 2007. http://articles.cnn.com/2007-05-07 /us/commentary.johnson_1_ hip-hop-misogynistic-images-music -videos?_s=PM:US.

Love, David A. "Hip-Hop and Politics Have a Long History Behind the Mic," theGrio.com, June 15, 2010. www.thegrio.com/specials /hip-hop-politics-from-the-beat-to-the-ballot/hip-hop-and-politics -have-a-long-history-behind-the-mic.php.

McWhorter, John H. "How Hip-Hop Holds Blacks Back," *City Journal*, Summer 2003. www.city-journal.org/html/13_3_how _hip_hop.html.

Poulton, Sonia. "Hip Hop and Violence: 'I Have to Ask Myself— Did I Help Promote Violence?,'" *Independent* (London), July 16, 2006. www.independent.co.uk/news/media/hip-hop-and-violence-i-have -to-ask-myself--did-i-help-promote-violence-407335.html.

Prison Culture. "Reversing Nihilism: Using Hip Hop to Empower Youth," December 5, 2011. www.usprisonculture.comblog/2011 /12/05/reversing-nihilism-using-hip-hop-to-empower-youth.

Saint Louis, Tai. "NC State U Study Connects Hip-Hop/Sexism," AllHipHop.com, February 22, 2008. http://allhiphop.com/2008 /02/22/nc-state-u-study-connects-hip-hopsexism.

Soderberg, Brandon, and Latoya Peterson. "Rap, Rape, and R&B: The Battle of the Sexes," *Spin*, Blogs, May 3, 2011. www.spin.com /articles/rap-rape-and-rb-battle-sexes.

Stewart, Justin T. "Nicki Minaj Speaks on Sexism in Hip-Hop," *Hip-Hop Wired*, November 5, 2009. http://hiphopwired.com /2009/11/05/nicki-minaj-speaks-on-sexism-in-hip-hop.

Tucker, Maria Luisa. "Where Politics and Hip Hop Collide," AlterNet, November 14, 2005. www.alternet.org/story/28118.

Washington, A. Scott. "Is Prison Culture Killing Our Children?," *Hip Hop Justice*. http://hiphopjustice.org/post/1314298727/is-prison -culture-killing-our-children.

Witherspoon, Chris. "Ashley Judd Defends Her Criticism of Hip-Hop," theGrio.com, April 11, 2011. www.thegrio.com/entertain ment/ashley-judd-defends-her-criticism-of-hip-hop-culture.php.

Websites

Hip-Hop Research Guide at Cornell University Library (http:// guides.library.cornell.edu/music3303). The Hip-Hop Research Guide is a webpage dedicated to hip-hop research at the Cornell University Library's website. The page includes books titles, videos, articles, links, photos, and other materials related to hip-hop research.

Media Awareness Network (www.media-awareness.ca/english/index .cfm). The Media Awareness Network is a nonprofit Canadian organization that promotes media literacy and understanding. Its website includes discussions of issues such as media violence and stereotyping, as well as news, blogs, and research.

Vibe (www.vibe.com). *Vibe* is a magazine devoted to rap music and hip-hop. Its website includes news from the magazine, blogs, videos, and other information related to rap business and culture.

Index

African American(s)
impact of 2008–2011
recession on, 94
imprisoned for marijuana
possession in California, 64
unemployment rates in Great
Recession for, *vs.* whites, *93*
young women, leading cause
of death among, 35
youth, cutbacks in after-
school programs and, 22
Aguilera, Christina, 79
Akinyele, 53
"All Of The Lights" (song), 75
Allende, Salvador, 85
America Works program, 95
American Bar Association, 34

Baldizon, Manuel, 28
Bambaata, Afrika, 85
Bascunan, Rodrigo, 12–13, 15
Beyoncé, 82
The Big Payback (Charnas), 106
Bill Haley and the Comets, *99*
"Bitches Ain't Sh--" (song), 53
Blackboard Jungle (film), 100
Boyd, Todd, 51
Brown, Chris, 40, 42, 43, *43,*
44, 71–72
Bufonk, 88–89
Bureau of Justice, 44
Bureau of Justice Statistics, 66

Bush (George W.)
administration, 95
Busta Rhymes, 72

Center for American Progress, 94
Center for Young Women's
Development, 43
Centers for Disease Control and
Prevention, 44
Chang, Jeff, 85
Charnas, Dan, 106
Chile
1973 coup d'etat in, 87
population below poverty line
in, *89*
rap/hip-hop as form of
political resistance in,
85–90
Christian Science Monitor
(newspaper), 48
Cole, Johnetta Betsch, 68
Combs, Sean "Puff Daddy,"
106, *107*
Control (album), 80
Cooper, Anderson, 9

Da Brat, 66–67
Daddy Yankee, *86*
Dating violence, percentage of
girls experiencing, by race, 44
Davis, Michaela Angela, 48–49,
50

De La Soul, 71
Dean, Terrance, 7
Denis, David, 16
Dj Erko, 86–87
Domestic violence
    rap community can come
        together to reject, 41–45
    rap music reflects an African
        American culture accepting
        of, 32–40
Donmillion, Alias, 15
Dr. Dre, 53
Dudley, Alex, 25
Dyson, Michael Eric, 92

Easy E, *13*
Elliot, Missy, *37, 38*
Eminem, 8, 75–76
Enter the Babylon System
    (Bascunan and Pearce), 12,
    14–15
Essence (magazine), Take Back
    the Music campaign of,
    48–50, 51, 62
Eve, 54

Fabolous, 75
Faith-Based and Community
    Initiatives program, 95
F.A.M.E. (album), 72
Fat Joe, 9
Female Chauvinist Pigs (Levy), 60
Feminism
    rap music has long tradition
        of, 52–58
    R&B music can teach lessons
        of, 77–82

1500 dias (music video), 85–86,
    87
50 Cent, *10,* 21, 22, 24, 67
Foxx, Jamie, 72, *73*
Funk, Liz, 59
Furious Five, 34

Game (formerly The Game), 9,
    22, 24
"Gangsta Gangsta" (song), 105
Gangsta rap, 12, 50, 105
"Ghetto Love" (song), 66
Gore, Tipper, 15
"Got Your Back" (song), 69
Gotti, Irv, 24
Great Recession (2008–2011),
    unemployment rates for
    blacks *vs.* whites in, *93,* 94
Guatemala, violence in, 27–28
Gun violence, rap music
    glamorizes/contributes to,
    11–15
Guy-Sheftall, Beverly, 49–50,
    51, 68

Haley, Bill and the Comets, *99,*
    100
Harris, Tameka "Tiny," *68*
Hiding in Hip Hop (Dean), 7
Hip-hop, 50
    in Chile, 86–89
    feminism in, 53–58
    first week albums sales for
        selected artists, *55*
    homophobia in, 7–9
    is mainstream, 18–20
    as reaction to oppression,
        33–34

Hip-Hop: Beyond Beats and Rhymes (Hurt), 60
Hip Hop Lives (album), 92
Homicide(s)/homicide rates
  drug-related, in Guatemala, 29
  in Latin America, by country, *30*
  as leading cause of death for young black women, 35
  of males, percentage change in, by race and year, *24*
Homophobia, 7–9
House Of Balloons (album), 72–73
Hurt, Byron, 60–61, *67*
Hustle and Flow (film), 17–18

"I Ain't Mad Atcha" (song), 36
"If" (song), 80–81
Industry Ears, Inc., 43

Ja Rule, 18–20
Jackson, Janet, 24, 78, 79–82, *81*
Jaffe, Sarah, 77
janet (album), 78, 81–82
Jara, Victor, 85
Jay-Z, 36–37, 75, 104, 108
Journal of Family Violence, 38
Judd, Ashley, 71
Jung, Carl, 33

Kane, Big Daddy, 8
Keyes, Cheryl, 92
Kinsella, Warren, 11

Kitwana, Bakari, 41, 54
KRS-One, 91, 92–94, 95–96, *96*

Lady B, 54
Lady Gaga, 9
Lah Tere, 89
Leach, Bryan, 25
Lee, Chris, 9
Left Eye (Lisa Lopes), 78
"Let's Talk About Sex" (song), 78
Levy, Ariel, 60
Lil B, 9
Lil' Kim, 22, 23, 38
Lil Wayne, 72
LL Cool J, *83*
Lopes, Lisa (Left Eye), 78
Love, Anyabwile, 7–8
"Love The Way You Lie" (song), 75–76
Lynette, Nicki, 56–58

Madonna, 81
M-Bone, *23*
Minaj, Nicki, 7, 56, *57*, 78
Marls, Marley, 92
The Massacre (album), 22
"Master P" (Percy Miller), 106
MC Lyte, 54
McWhorter, John H., 91
"Me and My Bitch" (song), 36, 38
Memoria Rebelde (music video), 87
"The Message" (song), 34–35
Minaj, Nicki, 8, 56, 78, 82

Miner, Natasha, 60
Missy Elliot, *37, 38*
Mister Cee, 7
Mitchell, Dreda Say, 98
"Monster" (song), 56
Moody, Nekesa Mumbi, 21
"Moon & the Stars" (song), 75
Morgan, Joan, 53–54, 55, 56
Morgan, Marcyliena, 55–56, 58
Murders. *See* Homicide(s)/
    homicide rates
"My Adidas" (song), 106

Native Tongues collective, 105
Neal, Mark Anthony, 39, 58
Nelly, 48, 53
Newsweek (magazine), 22
"No Bullshit" (song), 72
No! The Rape Documentary
    (film), 43
Nonviolence, rap music can be
    used to promote, 26–31
The Notorious B.I.G.
    (Christopher Wallace),
    22–23, 36, 38–39
Nueva Canción movement,
    88
NWA, 12, 105

Obama, Barack, 41, 42, 107–
    108
Odd Future, 74–75
Ofori-Atta, Akoto, 52
Oyewole, Abiodun, 62

Panteras Negras, 88
Pearce, Christian, 12

Perez Molina, Otto, 28, *28*
Pew Research Center, 44
Pimps Up, Hos Down (Sharpley-
    Whiting), 43
Piñera, Sebastian, 86
Pinkelman, Scott, 84
Pinochet, Augusto, 85, 87
Planeta Rock (hip-hop festival),
    85–86
Political views, of young voters,
    44
Portavoz, 87
Powell, Kevin, 38
Prison, incarceration rates by
    race/sex, *67*
Prison Culture (blog), 65
Public Enemy, 105
"Put It In Your Mouth" (song),
    53

Queen Latifah, 53, 54

R & B. *See* Rhythm and blues
    (R & B) music
Rap music
    can be used to promote
        nonviolence, 26–31
    contributes to worldwide
        harm to women, 47–51
    glamorizes/contributes to gun
        violence, 11–15
    has long tradition of
        feminism, 52–58
    is not politically thoughtful/
        effective, 91–97
    is worldwide form of political
        resistance, 84–90

misogynistic, men and women should reject, 59–64

no longer glamorizes prison, 16–20

promotion of capitalism/ success by
  is dangerous, 98–102
  is healthy, 103–108

R&B *vs.*, 71–72

reflects an African American culture accepting of domestic violence, 32–40

reflects/perpetuates culture of violence, 21–25

top selling albums, *63*

top songs with "Glock" in title, *14*

Rap performers, top earners among, *105*

Ready4Work program, 95

Rebel Diaz, 89

"The Revolution Will Not Be Televised" (song), 105

Rhythm and blues (R&B) music
  can teach feminist lessons, 77–82
  is more harmful to women than rap, 70–76

Rhythm Nation 1814 (album), 80

Rihanna, 40, 42, 43, 44, 71, 72, 75

Robyn, 82

"Rock Around the Clock" (song), 100

Routledge, Paul, 104

Run-D.M.C., 106

Sade, 75

Saldana, Zoe, 67

Salt-n-Pepa, 78

Scott, Jill, *49*

Scott-Heron, Gil, 104–105

Sepulveda, Monse, 26

Sexual assaults, women victims of, relationships between attackers and, *74*

Shakur, Tupac, 18, 22–23, 36, 54

Sharpley-Whiting, Tracy, 43

Sharpton, Al, 22, 24–25, 63

Simmons, Aishah, 43

Simmons, Russell, *46*

Sims, Brian, 32

60 Minutes (TV program), 8

Social learning theory, 34–35

Soderberg, Brandon, 70

"Song Cry" (song), 36–37

Spears, Britney, 79

Subverso, 87

Take Back the Music campaign (*Essence* magazine), 48, 51, 62

Tatchell, Peter, 8

"That's the Way Love Goes" (song), 78

T.I., *17,* 18, *19, 68, 69*

Tijoux, Anita, 88

"Tip-Drill" (song), 48, 53

TLC, 78

"To the Beat Y'all" (song), 54

Trasciende, 26, 29–31

"21 Questions" (song), 67

Tyler, the Creator, 75
2Pac, 18, 36. *See also* Shakur, Tupac

United States
   distribution of wealth in, *101*
   music genre preferences in, *79*
   numbers of incarcerated persons in, by ethnicity/gender, *67*
"U.N.I.T.Y." (song), 53
Universal Music Group, 25

Voters, political views of young *vs.* older, 44

Wallace, Christopher. *See* The Notorious B.I.G.
Wealth, distribution of, in US, *101*
The Weeknd, 72–75
Weisstuch, Liza, 47

Welfare reform, 94
West, Kanye, 7, 75, 92, 104
"What Have You Done For Me Lately" (song), 80
"Wicked Games" (song), 73–74
Women
   hip-hop prison culture hurts, 65–69
   loyalty of, as construct in rap music, 36–37, 68–69
   rap music contributes to worldwide harm to, 47–51
   R&B music is more harmful to than rap, 70–76
Wright, Darren, 104

Yates, Steve, 103
Year Up program, 94–95
"You Be Killin' Em" (song), 75

Zirin, Dave, 92
Zulu Nation, 85

Picture Credits

© AP Images, 86

© AP Images/Shawn Baldwin, 46

© AP Images/Tina Fineberg, 83

© AP Images/Shiho Fukada, 107

© AP Images/Scott Gries/PictureGroup via AP Images, 96

© AP Images/Tim Johnson, 49

© AP Images/Keystone/Alessandro Della Bella, 37

© AP Images/John Minchillo, 57

© AP Images/Chris Pizzello, 43

© AP Images/PRNewsFoto/BET Networks, Jeff Daly/
  PictureGroup, 17

© AP Images/Gregory Smith, 68

© AP Images/Mark J. Terrill, 81

© Frederick M. Brown/Getty Images, 61

© Rick Diamond/Wire Image, 73

© John Franks/Keystone/Getty Images, 99

© Jason Kempin/FilmMagic/Getty Images, 13

© Brenda Ann Kenneally/Corbis, 10

© Saul Martinez/EPA/Landov, 28

© Mark Ralston/AFP/Getty Images, 23

Steve Zmina, 14, 24, 30, 55, 63, 67, 74, 79, 89, 93, 101, 105